Table of Contents

INSTRUCTOR'S MANUAL

ROSANNE J. MAREK

Ball State University

THE
WORLD'S HISTORY

COMBINED EDITION

HOWARD SPODEK

PRENTICE HALL, *Upper Saddle River, New Jersey 07458*

© 1998 by PRENTICE-HALL, INC.
Simon & Schuster / A Viacom Company
Upper Saddle River, New Jersey 07458

ISBN 0-13-644477-6
Printed in the United States of America

Chapter One: The Dry Bones Speak

Chapter Outline

A. Human Origins in Myth and History

    1. Early Myths

        a. Akkad

        b. India

        c. West Asia

    2. The function of creation myths

B. Evolutionary Explanations of Human Origins

C. Piecing Together the Evolutionary Record: <u>How do we know?</u>

    1. Neanderthals

    2. *Homo Erectus*

    3. *Ausralopithicus africanus*

    4. *Homo habilis*

    5. *Australopithicus afarensis* ("Lucy")

    6. *Australopithicus ramidus*

    7. *Homo sapiens*

    8. African origin

D. Reading the Genetic Record

E. Cultural Change and Biological Change

F. Key Questions Remaining

G. The Theory of Scientific Revolution

H. Humans Create Culture

I. How Did We Survive? <u>How do we know?</u>

    1. Dating archaeological finds

    2. Global migration

    3. Increased population and new settlements

    4. Changes in the tool kit

        a. stone tools

        b. "women's tools, women's work"

J. Cave Art and Portable Art

K. Language and Communication

L. Agriculture: from Hunter-Gatherer to Farmer

Chapter Summary

This chapter discusses some of the early creation myths. One of the oldest is **Enuma Elish**, which dates back to almost 2000 B.C.E. It gave meaning and direction to human life and affirmed the authority of the powerful priestly class. The ancient Indian epic of **Rigveda** dates from about 1000 B.C.E. This myth supports the hierarchical organization in India's historic caste system. Perhaps the most widely known creation myth is told in the book of **Genesis** in the Hebrew Bible. Genesis assigns humans a unique and privileged place as the final crown and master of creation. For thousands of years, these and other creation myths presented people with explanations of their place in the world, their relationship to the gods, to the rest of creation, and to one another.

By the mid-1700s, some European philosophers and natural scientists challenged the Bible's story of individual, special creation of each life form. Challenging the biblical account required a new method of inquiry. In the mid-eighteenth century, these new forms began to emerge. Finally, **Charles Darwin** and **Alfred Russel Wallace** separately formulated the modern theory of the biological evolution of species.

Both Darwin and Wallace reached their conclusions as a result of extensive travel overseas. In 1856, they published a joint paper on the basic concepts of evolution. In 1859, Darwin published his findings and conclusions in *On the Origin of the Species by Means of Natural Selection*, a book that forever altered humankind's conception of itself. In 1871, Darwin published *The Descent of Man*, which extended his argument to the evolution of humans.

The chapter summarizes the early discoveries by scientists of **hominids**, the ancestors and relatives of early humans which emerged as the human line branched off from apes. Between 1945 and 1955, several scientists discovered bone tools among the hominid fossils.

The work of modern scientists such as **Louis**, **Mary**, and **Richard Leakey**, and **Donald Johanson** is also cited in Chapter One. In 1959, Louis and Mary Leakey discovered **Zinj**, an Australopithecus who was 1.75 million years old. He was a hominid closer to apes than to modern humans. Continued excavations at **Olduvai** turned up skull fragments of creatures which the Leakeys named **Homo habilis**, "handy person," because of the stone tools they manufactured and used in scavenging, hunting, and butchering food. In the 1970s their son, Richard, discovered additional bones of the species Homo habilis. The finds confirmed the size of its brain, its opposable thumb, and its upright, bipedal walk.

In Ethiopia, in 1974, Donald Johanson discovered "Lucy," the first known representative of **Australopithecus afarensis**. The discovery pushed back the date of the earliest known hominid to about 3.2 million years B.C.E.

The earliest known **Homo sapiens** (human, wise) fossil was discovered in 1967 - 68 on the coast of South Africa. In the search for the time and place of the origins of Homo sapiens, discoveries based on genetics and laboratory research emerged about two decades ago. Scientists began to study the DNA record of human and animal genes. DNA, the protein building block within each living cell, reveals the degrees of similarity and difference among the creatures studied.

In addition to the physiological changes favored by natural selection, hominids began to shape their environment through cultural activities. Homo sapiens, like homo erectus before them, migrated and spread over the entire earth, except for the polar regions. Unlike their predecessors, however, they developed forms of symbolic expression–apparently spiritual and cultural in nature–including burial rites, and artwork. These cultural forms suggest that about 35,000 years ago, the human brain (but not the rest of human physiology) went through some further evolutionary development. Homo sapiens evolved into **Homo sapiens sapiens** (wise, wise, human). Finally, early humans learned to domesticate animals. By 15,000 – 10,000 B.C.E., humans had the biological and cultural capacity to farm and raise animals. A permanent source of food to eat, or materials to trade, might have outweighed the desire to shift with the seasons and travel with the herds.

Chapter One also studies the development of language. Modern language provided the ability to communicate with others on an individual basis. It allowed for increasingly sophisticated internal thought and reflection. The sophisticated psychological and social relationships that make us human became possible only with the development of language.

Perhaps rising population pressures left humans no alternative. Scope for travel was restricted by the press of neighbors. On limited land, hunter-gatherers found that planting their own crops and domesticating their own animals could provide them with more food than hunting and gathering. Despite the risks of weather and of plant and animal diseases that left agricultural settlements vulnerable, some groups began to settle. Ten thousand years ago, almost all humans lived by hunting and gathering. Two thousand years ago, most were farmers or herders. Moreover, in the midst of this transformation (which created the first agricultural villages), cities, too, grew up as the central administrative, economic, and religious centers of their regions.

Learning Objectives

After students have read and studies Chapter One, they should be able to:

1. Explain the physical characteristics of Australopithecus, Homo habilis, Homo erectus, Homo sapiens, and Homo sapiens sapiens.
2. Discuss the effects of the agricultural revolution on the environment and the culture of early humans.
3. Explain why the development of language is one of humanity's most significant achievements.
4. Locate on a world map the sites where the remains of hominids and early humans were found.
5. Explain how the invention of tools influenced the culture of early humans.

Suggestions for Lecture Topics

1. Discuss the importance of spoken language in the cultural development of early humans.
2. Explain the importance of the agricultural revolution.
3. Point out that shifts in the world's climate caused evolutionary changes in humans and other species.
4. Discuss the major differences between humans and primates.

Topics for Essays or Class Discussion

1. Summarize the creation myths. What do they tell us about early humans?
2. Do recent scientific findings support or disprove creation myths?
3. Discuss the similarities and differences between humans and apes.
4. Explain the relationship between the discoveries of the Leakeys and Darwin's hypotheses, published in *On the Origin of Species by Means of Natural Selection*, and *The Descent of Man*.

Vocabulary

paleoanthropology	*The Descent of Man*
archeologists	Charles Darwin
Vishnu	Homo erectus
On the Origin of Species by Means of Natural Selection	Homo sapiens
Homo habilis	Richard Leakey
Homo sapiens sapiens	Mary Leakey
Louis Leakey	Olduvai Gorge
Donald Johanson	"Lucy"
hominid	DNA

Audio-Visual Resources

Mysteries of Mankind: **National Geographic Society, 1988. 60 minutes, color.**

In this segment of the Emmy award-winning series, scientists analyzing fossil remains and utilizing modern technologies unravel the mysteries of human origins.

In Search of Human Origins: **NOVA, WGBH Boston, 1994. 3 VHS videos, 60 minutes each, color.**

In this exciting new series, famed anthropologist David Johanson studies the evolutionary path from apes to humans. In Part I, he discusses "Lucy," a hominid who lived over three million years ago. In Part II, he considers Homo habilis and Homo erectus. In Part III, he investigates the possible links between Homo erectus, Neanderthals, and modern humans.

Additional Text Resources

Maps:

Human Ancestors (7)

Early Humans in the Ice Age (23)

The colonization of the Pacific (24)

Features:

Gender Issues and Cultural Evolution (20)

Spotlight:

Picturing Neanderthals (8)

Chapter Two: From Village Community to City State

Chapter Outline

A. Food First: the Agricultural Village

    1. Basic Crops and livestock

    2. Neolithic tools, products, and trade

B. The First Cities

C. The Meaning of Cities

D. Sumer

    1. Sumer: <u>What do we know?</u>

        a. the birth of the city

        b. size

        d. civic loyalty

        e. leadership and the state

        f. religion: the priesthood and the "Cosmo-magical" city

        g. occupational specialization and class structure

        h. arts and invention

        i. trade and markets: wheeled cart and sailboat

        j. monumental architecture and adornment

        k. writing and literature

    2. Sumer: <u>How do we know?</u>

        a. cuneiform script

        b. the *Epic of Gilgamesh*

        c. the *Code of Hammurabi*

E. Early Urbanization: Some Modern Critiques

    1. Lewis Mumford

    2. Karl Marx

    3. Gerda Lerner

F. Mythistory

Chapter Summary

Until about 12,000 years ago, humans hunted and gathered their food following the migrations of animals and the seasonal cycles of the crops. They established temporary base camps for their activities, and caves served as homes and meeting places, but they had not established permanent settlements. They had begun to domesticate some animals, especially the dog and the sheep, but they had not yet begun the systematic practice of agriculture. Then, beginning in about 10,000 B.C.E., people began to settle down, constructing the first agricultural villages.

The first agricultural villages that archaeologists have discovered date to about 10,000 B.C.E., and are located in the **fertile crescent**. By 8000 B.C.E., the **Natufians**, named for their valley in northern Israel, and the peoples immediately to the south, in the Jordan River Valley near **Jericho**, were growing fully domesticated cereals. Peas and lentils, and other pulses and legumes followed. The peoples of the fertile crescent hunted gazelles and goats. Later, they domesticated the goat and the sheep. In Turkey, they added pigs; around the Mediterranean, cattle.

In other parts of the world, agriculture and animal domestication focused on other varieties. In the western hemisphere, these included **maize** (especially in Mesoamerica), and root crops such as **manioc** and **sweet potatoes** in South America. Amerindians domesticated the llama, guinea pig, and the turkey. Domesticated dogs probably accompanied their migrant masters across the Bering Straits about 15,000 years ago. Perhaps the process of domestication was then repeated with the dogs found in the Americas.

In southeast Asia and in tropical Africa, wild roots and tubers, including yams, were the staple crops. In the Vindhya Mountain areas of central India, rice was among the first cultivated, rather than just being harvested from the wild in southeast and east Asia, but a date similar to India's seems likely. Our knowledge of early agriculture continues to grow as the archaeological record is expanded and revised. European sedentary agriculture, for example, which was once thought to have been borrowed from the Near East, may have been a local response to changing climate conditions.

The era in which villages took form is usually named **Neolithic**, or New Stone Age—named for its tools rather than its crops. Archaeological digs from Neolithic villages abound with blades, knives, sickles, arrows, daggers, spears, fish hooks and harpoons, mortars and pestles, and rudimentary plows and hoes.

The first cities were constructed on the economic base of sedentary village agriculture communities. The earliest city dwellers advanced their skills in metallurgy, and products of their craftsmanship in copper, tin, and their alloys abound in archaeological excavations. In recognition of these technical breakthroughs, we often call the era of the first cities the **Bronze Age**.

External relations with other cities required skilled negotiations and a diplomatic corps emerged. Armies mobilized for defense and attack. In short, with the growth of the city, the early state was also born with its specialized organization, centralized rule, and powerful armies.

By about 3300 B.C.E. in **Sumer**, which is geographically equivalent to today's southern Iraq, the world's first system of writing evolved. It is one of the revolutionary inventions in all of human history.

After some 200 years under **Akkadian** rule, the **Mesopotamian** city-states regained independance and resumed their inter-urban warfare until about 1750 B.C.E., when **Hammurabi** of Babylon dealt them a final defeat and the Sumerian peoples began to vanish from history. The cities they had built—Kish, Uruk, Ur, Nippur, Umma, and dozens of smaller ones—died out, having fought each other to exhaustion. The Sumerian legacy lived on, however, absorbed into the literature, philosophy, religion, law, and new patterns of urbanization of their conquerors.

For the Sumerians, the size and elegance of their cities and monuments was a source of great pride. Despite their accomplishments, the Sumerians and their literature were lost to history for at least 2000 years. The locations of even the greatest of the historic sites passed from memory until they were recovered in the late nineteenth century.

The Sumerians had invented **cuneiform** writing—using reed styluses to make wedge-like forms on clay tablets. Later conquerors had adopted this script for writing Akkadian, Assyrian, and Babylonian. The conquest of **Alexander the Great**, however, helped to introduce the more functional **Aramaic** alphabet, and cuneiform died out. The last known cuneiform text had been written in 75 C.E.

Much of what we know about the ancient Sumerian imagination and world vision comes from its greatest literary work; a series of tales about the great hero **Gilgamesh**, which were woven together in *The Epic of Gilgamesh*. A second form of written document that marks the evolution to a more complex society is the legal code. Archaeologists discovered at Ur, fragments of a legal code that dates to the twenty-first century B.C.E., indicating the usage of such codes at a time much earlier than the time frame when these fragments may have been written. Legal systems remained crucial for all Mesopotamian urban societies, and the post-Sumerian code of the Babylonian king Hammurabi (about 1750 B.C.E. but rediscovered to the modern world only in 1901-02), seems to have been built on the earlier concepts.

The transformation of society from a rural, egalitarian, kin-based one to an urban, hierarchical, territorial, and class-based one may have provided the entering wedge for the subordination of women. Women in Sumer were generally given basic rights, including the rights to hold property, engage in business, and serve as legal witnesses.

From the time of Sumer, the political questions—questions of the organizations and administration of the polis or city-state in order to achieve a good life—have been central to the process of urbanization. In Sumer, the answers depended on the king and the priests. In the next two chapters we will see how these questions and answers evolved in other primary cities and city-states around the world.

Learning Objectives

After students have read and studied Chapter Two, they should be able to:

1. Explain the relationship between the systematic practice of agriculture and the development of agricultural villages.
2. Know that the first agricultural villages date to about 10,000 B.C.E., and are located in the fertile crescent.
3. Understand that in Mesopotamia, the Sumerians pioneered the world's first urban revolution.
4. Recognize that the Sumerians' invention of writing altered the entire course of human history.
5. Know that Hammurabi, the great king of Babylon, in the first known ruler to have created a detailed legal code.

Suggestions for Lecture Topics

1. List the technologies which were developed in the Neolithic Age.
2. Outline the religious beliefs held by early humans.
3. Point out the relationships between geography and history--particularly when studying early civilizations.
4. Discuss several ways the early peoples interacted with their environment.

Topics for Essays or Class Discussion

1. Explain why the Agricultural Revolution was a turning point in history.
2. Discuss the basic characteristics of a civilization.
3. How did advancing civilizations lead to a more stratified society?
4. How did the development of cities transform human life?

Vocabulary

fertile crescent

Neolithic Age

Industrial Revolution

Sumer

Semites

ziggurats

The Epic of Gilgamesh

cuneiform writing

Code of Hammurabi

city-states

Audio-Visual Resources

The Agricultural Revolution: 1985. 26 minutes, color.

Examines the role of agriculture in the development of the village communities which became the foundation of later civilizations.

Additional Text Resources

Maps:

The Fertile Crescent (36)

Farming in China (39)

The spread of civilizations (40)

Mesopotamian trade (46)

Document Extracts:

Features:

Spotlight:

Chapter Three: River Valley Civilizations

Chapter Outline

A. Introduction: the Rise of Cities and States along the Nile and Indus

    1. Comparisons with Mesopotamian city-states

    2. Comparisons between Egypt and the Indus valley

B. Egypt: the "Gift of the Nile"

    1. Earliest Egypt: <u>How do we know?</u>

        a. hieroglyphics and the Rosetta Stone

        b. writing: inventing it, deciphering it

        c. archaeological excavations

    2. Earliest Egypt: <u>What do we know?</u>

        a. Upper and Lower Egypt: Narmer

        b. god-kings and *ma'at*

        c. ancient Egyptian dynasties

        d. the cities

            i. the *nomes*

            ii. irrigation systems

            iii. the debate over city-states in earliest Egypt

            iv. purposes of the cities: Aketaten (Amarna)

        e. the state and its architecture: the Old Kingdom

            i. the tomb of Djoser

            ii. the pyramids

        f. from state to empire

            i. the Middle Kingdom spreads into Nubia

            ii. invasions of the Hyksos and the fall of the Middle Kingdom

C. The Indus Valley Civilization and its Mysteries

    1. Harappa and Mohenjo-Daro

    2. The Indus Valley: <u>How do we know?</u>

        a. archaeological excavations

        b. age and extent of the civilization

        c. Harappan civilization and Mesopotamia

        d. the lack of written records

3. The Indus Valley: <u>What do we know?</u>

    a. the bureaucratic governments

    b. the plan of the cities

    c. crafts and trade: cotton

    d. Harappan civilization and the Aryans

4. Legacies of the Indus Valley on Indian civilization

Chapter Summary

Two urban civilizations flanked Mesopatamia: the **Nile Valley** to the southwest, and the **Indus Valley** to the southeast. Scholarly opinion is divided as to whether these two city systems learned to build cities and states from the Mesopotamian example or if they invented them independently. Whatever the truth, peoples of these three river valleys created quite separate and distinct patterns of urbanization and political life.

In the **Tigris-Euphrates Valley**, development of the physical city and the institutional state went hand-in-hand. In the Nile Valley, the creation of the **Egyptian** state had greater significance than the growth of individual cities. In the Indus Valley, we have extensive archaeological information on the cities, but know next to nothing about the formation of states. Until scholars learn to decipher the script and language of the Indus civilization, our knowledge of their institutional development will remain limited.

During its 5000 years of recorded history, Egypt was conquered and ruled by several different civilizations. Egypt has undergone so many political and cultural transformations over such a very long time, that its earliest indigenous roots are difficult to uncover.

Modern Egyptology was born when the **Rosetta Stone** was discovered in 1799, and later translated. Archaeological excavations, primarily for monumental objects, began in 1858, although tomb-robbing and theft of ancient artifacts had been continous from earliest times. By about 1900, scholars had identified the basic outlines of Egypt's history from approximately 3600 B.C.E. to their own time.

By 12,000 B.C.E., residents of **Nubia** and Upper Egypt were using stones to grind local wild grapes into food, and by 8000 B.C.E., flour was prepared from their seeds. By 6000 B.C.E., the first traces of the cultivation of wheat and barley, grasses and cereals, and of the domestication of sheep and goats appeared. Between 4000 and 3000 B.C.E., the bronze age began in Egypt, as the new metal was used in tools and weapons. Population increased, as did the size of new villages, and by 3300 B.C.E., the first walled towns appeared in the upper Nile. By 2700 B.C.E., Egypt exhibited the cultural complexity associated with early civilizations, including a national religious ideology, and the centralized control of political administration, and even of artistic productivity.

In 2649 – 2695 B.C.E., **King Djoser** had a **mastaba** built to hold his remains at death. This forerunner of the **pyramids** shows an astonishing royal control over labor, finances, and architectural and building techniques. The administrative organization and economic productivity of government continued to increase until, by the end of this dynasty, Egypt had extended its control over the Nile as far south as the first cataract, its classical southern frontier. At the same time, Egypt's artistic genius continued to develop in the sculpture of its tombs, and the sophistication of its script.

In 2575 – 2465 B.C.E., the kings supervised the construction of the greatest pyramids in history. The 450 foot (137 meter) high pyramids of **Khufu** (Cheops; r. 2551 – 2528) and of **Khefren** (r. 2520 – 2494), and the smaller pyramid of **Menkaure** (r. 2490 – 2472), all arranged in a cluster with the **Sphinx**, proclaim aspiration to immortality, creative vision, and organizational power.

Belief in one god (**Aten**, represented by the sun) was promoted during the reign of **Akhenaton** (c. 1353 – 1337), when the capital of Egypt was moved from **Thebes** to **El-Amarna**. At other times, the Egyptians worshipped a pantheon.

The **Middle Empire** was overthrown by foreign invaders. They were called **Hyksos**, or "ruler of foreign lands," and little is known of their origins or their rule. When Egyptian kings arose and expelled the Hyksos in about 1532 B.C.E., Egypt began its **New Kingdom**.

The civilization of the Indus Valley was rediscovered only in the 1920s. By now archaeologists have identified over 1000 settlement sites of this civilization distributed over more than 400,000 square miles (1 million square kilometers), making it the most widespread civilization of its time.

In the later half of the nineteenth century and the first half of the twentieth, the excavations of **Marshall** and **Banerji** uncovered an urban civilization that had been lost for thousands of years. Before these excavations, scholars had believed that the civilization of **India** had begun in the **Ganges Valley** with the arrival of **Aryan** invaders from Persia or central Asia in about 1250 B.C.E. and the construction of their first cities in about 700 B.C.E. The discovery of the **Harappan** cities pushed the origin of Indian civilization back an additional 1500 years and located it in an entirely different ecological zone.

Written records, the key that re-opened the civilizations of ancient Mesopotamia and Egypt, are missing in the Indus. The only written materials discovered so far are seal inscriptions, which give only limited information, and thus far, even they have not been interpreted satisfactorily. Scholars such as **Akso Pranpola** seem to have found some specific names and dates on the seals, but these interpretations are disputed. Without the written records, we are limited in our understanding of Indus civilization. Artifactual remains give a good representation of the physical cities and settlements, but not of their institutions. Moreover, while we can guess at the function and meaning of the artifacts and physical structures remaining from our own perspective, we do not have the works of the people themselves to explain their own understanding of their civilization.

Archeological evidence to date reveals an urban civilization with its roots beginning as early as 7000 B.C.E. By about 2500 B.C.E., a thriving civilization had reached and maintained its apex for about 500 years. The regularity of plan and construction suggest a government with great organizational and bureaucratic capacity, but there is no truly monumental architecture to mark clearly the presence of a palace or temple. And there is little sign of social stratification in the plan or buildings.

Newer archaeological evidence suggests that the decline, de-urbanization, and dispersal of the Indus civilization seems to have preceded the Aryan invasion. Further evidence suggests that the Aryans may not have swept into the region in a single all-conquering expedition, but in a series of smaller waves. The arrival of the Aryans may have only completed the Harappa decay.

Four legacies of Harappan stand out. First, the Aryan invaders were a nomadic group, who must have employed at least some of the arts of settlement and civilization from the already settled residents. Second, as newcomers to the ecological zones of India, the Aryans must also have learned methods of farming and animal husbandry from the Harappans. Third, similarities between a three-headed figure frequently appearing in Harappan seals, and later representations of the Aryan god **Siva** suggest that an earlier Harappan god may have been adopted and adapted by the Aryans.

Finally, the Aryan **caste** system, which ranks people at birth according to occupation, color, and ritual purity, and prescribes for them the people with whom they may enter into social intercourse and marriage, may reflect the need of the Aryans to regulate relationships between themselves and the Harappans. In order to claim and maintain their own supremacy, the Aryans elaborated the social structures of the caste system and relegated the native inhabitants to permanent low status within it.

Learning Objectives

After students have read and studied Chapter Three, they should be able to:

1. Know that during its 5000 years of recorded history, Egypt was conquered and ruled by several different civilizations.
2. Understand the significance of the Rosetta Stone.
3. Be able to list some of the achievements of ancient Egypt.
4. Understand that because we lack written records, we are limited in our understanding of the Indus civilization.

Suggestions for Lecture Topics

1. Emphasize the role of rivers in the formation of the Nile and Indus civilizations.
2. List the conditions in the Nile and Indus River Valleys which fostered the development of civilization.
3. Summarize the major time periods in ancient Egypt.

Topics for Essays or Class Discussion

1. Explain how the government and religion were linked in ancient Egypt. Does religion influence government?
2. Discuss the role of technology in the development of civilization.
3. How did civilizations lead to a more complex system of social classes?

Vocabulary

Mesopotamia

Tigris-Euphrates Valley

dynasty

hieroglyphs

Rosetta Stone

papyrus

shaduf irrigation

Hyksos

Indus River

Harappans

Audio-Visual Resources

The Pyramids and the Cities of the Pharoahs: 1995. 75 minutes, color.
Portrays Egypt's awakening over 5,000 years ago.

Additional Text Resources

Maps:

Land of the Nile (62)

Cities of the Indus (73)

City of the Plain (Mohenjo-Daro) (77)

Document Extracts:

The Story of Si-nuhe and the Glorification of Court and Capital (70)

The Egyptian *Book of the Dead* and the "Negative Confession" (71)

Features:

The Legend of Isis, Osiris, and Horus (67)

Spotlight:

Writing: Inventing It, Deciphering It (60)

Chapter Four: A Polycentric World

Chapter Outline

A. Introduction: Cities and States in East Asia, West Africa, and the Americas

B. China: the Xia, Shang, and Zhou Dynasties

    1. Earliest times: <u>How do we know?</u>

        a. texts

        b. oracle bones

        c. archaeology

    2. Earliest times: <u>What do we know?</u>

        a. the earliest villages

        b. historical evidence of the Xia Dynasty

        c. similarities among the three dynasties

    3. City and state under the Shang

        a. the "Cosmo-magical" city

        b. Anyang, the last Shang capital

C. West Africa: the Niger River Valley

    1. West Africa before urbanization

    2. Jenne Jeno: <u>How do we know?</u>

    3. State formation

    4. Later states and empires

D. The Western Hemisphere: Mesoamerica and South America

    1. Origins, migration, and agriculture

    2. Mesoamerican urbanization

        a. Olmec civilization along the Gulf Coast

        b. Zapotec civilization in the Oaxaca Valley

        c. Teotihuacan in the Valley of Mexico

        d. Toltec civilization in the Valley of Mexico

        e. Aztec civilization in the Valley of Mexico

        f. Mayan civilization: <u>How do we know?</u>

            i. Mayan cities

            ii. Mayan script

            iii. the *Popul Vuh*

        g. Mayan civilization: <u>What do we know?</u>

3. Urbanization in South America

    a. coastal settlements and networks

        i. the Moche

        ii. the Chimu

    b. urbanization in the Andes Mountains

        i. the Chavin

        ii. Tiwanaku, Huari, and Nazca

        iii. the Inca

E. Agricultural Towns of North America

Chapter Summary

This chapter chronicles the origin and nature of the first seven urbanized areas in the world. Historical and archaeological sources are offered to explain these cultures. Various reasons for the locations and movement of these early populations is explored, as well as their driving forces. Both power structure and politics, religion and belief systems are revealed. A timeline is utilized to further explain important hallmarks in the areas of politics, architecture and artifacts, literature and religion, and social development. The historical and archaeological studies used to piece together these cultures are clearly explained.

Three early dynasties of northern **China** (as early as 1700 B.C.E.) were based around the **Yellow River Valley**. Each ruled over the most powerful kingdoms of their time. Once thought to be successive in time, this chapter reveals more recent evidence suggesting that there was an overlap in the timelines of the **Xia**, **Shang**, and **Zhou** dynasties. The leadership and economics of these groups is explored, as well as spiritual beliefs and practices. A rich source of knowledge surfaced in the late 1800s and early 1900s with the discovery of over 100,000 examples of "oracle bones." These were bones of various animals and turtle shells which were used for religious ceremonies and foretelling the future. Many were inscribed with names and dates of rulers. Archeologists have also revealed such things as pottery, burial practices, warfare, and metallurgical and agricultural practices. Many of these related to trade and economic practices as well as political and power distribution. One page of the chapter describes these ancient rites as "**cosmo-magical**." These cities are said to have begun as ritual centers. Diviners were important people here, sometimes calling for human sacrifices. Armies were maintained that took prisoners for sacrificing.

The chapter then looks at the **Niger River Valley** (from 400 C.E.) of **West Africa** to characterize urban life in three of the first cities there--**Timbuktu**, **Jenne**, and **Mopti**. The transitions from village life to city dwelling are illustrated. Evidence is given here of such things as: language and technology skill, trade, worship centers, diet, jewelry, and agricultural and nomadic origins. The chapter shows the importance of iron smelting--appearing in West Africa around 500 B.C.E.--and its evidence of influences from other cultures. Agriculture contributed to the basis of trade, which promoted expansion and urbanization. Trade based empires arose, enhanced by new trade routes.

In the next part of the chapter, the first cities of the Western hemisphere are compared and contrasted to those of Asia and Africa. The **Olmec** was the earliest (1500 B.C.E.) of these societies. They had origins as cosmo-magical shrine centers, having far-reaching influence over the customs of distant cultures on the continent. They served important functions in rule and trade, as well as religion. Geographic differences are given for their choice of locating near coastal areas, rather than inland rivers. Also apparent is the lack of iron in this culture. Construction and transportation methods were very labor intensive in this area. These cities of the Western hemisphere did not create a writing system, with the exception of the **Maya**. The chapter concludes with a discussion of coastal settlements of **South America** and urbanization in the **Andes Mountains**.

Learning Objectives

After students have read and studied Chapter Four, they should be able to:

1. Describe the factors contributing to urbanization in the earliest cities.
2. Explain the role of religion in these early cultures regarding political and economic life.
3. Suggest reasons for the geographic locations of settlements in Asia and West Africa, and be able to compare and contrast with those in the Western hemisphere.
4. Give examples of how archaeological evidence can explain class systems and political power in these cities.
5. Describe how trade with outside peoples is demonstrated by archaeological evidence.
6. Explain the role of levees and canals for those cities along the Yellow River.
7. Give two examples of similarities between the first cities of the Americas and those studied in either Asia or Africa.
8. Briefly describe the migration pattern of people in the Western hemisphere.
9. Give one example of a farming practice that forced people to keep moving.
10. Offer a reasonable explanation as to why the city of Teotihuacan was intentionally destroyed by fire in 650 C.E.

Suggestions for Lecture Topics

1. Explain the term cosmo-magical and how it relates to cultures and their hierarchy. Stress the powers of the diviners over the people and their futures.
2. Talk of metallurgy and its role in the cultures, explaining how archaeologists could tell when it evolved within a culture and when it was introduced from outside a culture.
3. Discuss the role of trade in establishing the urban living arrangement. Explain the importance of trade as it relates to agricultural practices and labor.
4. Explain the evidence of the political power structure and its relationship to: the establishment of cities, trade, spiritual life of people, agricultural methods, taxation, military.
5. Review the commonalities of the earliest urban lifestyle and its parallels with modern day life.
6. Discuss the role of migration in early time and how it became a way of life for some societies due to their agricultural methods. Discuss the role it played, and its limitations and advantages. Show how it was replaced by other ways of living and suggest both advantages and disadvantages to both ways of life.

Topics for Essay or Class Discussion

1. What characteristics did all of the cities described in Chapter Four have in common?
2. Describe the importance of the belief system for the survival of the people in these ancient cities. Draw parallels with modern day. Is there more need now or less? Why or why not?
3. What chances did lower-class Gulf Coast people have to improve their position in life? How would you deal with a life like theirs?
4. Could the lives of some of the people be described as slavery? Can you imagine slavery by another name? What are some different versions of slavery? Do you see any examples in modern North American society to compare?

Vocabulary

zimbabwes

Huang Ho River valley

Yangshao

Longshan

Timbuktu

Jenne-Jeno

Olmec

Shang Dynasty

Teotihuacan

Inca

Maya

Oracle Bones

Audio-Visual Resources

Legacy: **Ambrose Video Publishing Co., 1991. 57 minutes, color.**
This six-part series explores the influence of ancient cultures on our lives today.

Additional Text Resources
Maps:

Shang China (83)

Trade across the Sahara (88)

The spread of Bantu (92)

Classic cultures of the Americas (96)

Teotihuacán (98)

Document Extracts:

The Popol Vuh (102)

Features:

The Cosmo-magical City (86)

Agricultural Towns of North America (103)

Spotlight:

Shang Dynasty Tombs (90)

Chapter Five: Dawn of the Empires

Chapter Outline

A. The Meaning of Empire

    1. Characteristics of empires

    2. Hegemony and dominance

    3. Causes of the decline and fall of empires

B. The Earliest Empires

    1. Mesopotamia and the "Fertile Crescent"

        a. Sargon of Akkad

        b. Babylonian empires

    2. Egypt and international conquest

    3. the Assyrians

    4. Egypt under occupation

C. Persia

    1. The rise of Persia

    2. Imperial policies

        a. Cyrus II (the Great)

        b. Cambyses II

        c. Darius I

    3. Persepolis: imperial capital

D. Greek City-States: Reality and Image

    1. Minoans and Mycenaeans: the earliest city-states of the Aegean

    2. The Persian Wars

    3. Athens: from city-state to mini-empire

        a. the city of Athens

        b. historical background to Athenian democracy

    4. The Greek city-state in art, literature, and philosophy

    5. Pericles and Socractes on Athenian democracy

E. The Limits of City-State Democracy

    1. <u>How do we know?</u> <u>What do we know?</u>

    2. Was classical Athens a "phallocracy?"

    3. Athens becomes an imperial power: the Peloponnesian War

F. The Empire of Alexander the Great

    1. The rise of Macedonia

    2. The campaigns of Alexander

    3. The legacy of Alexander: the Hellenistic ecumene

Chapter Summary

This chapter discusses the development of **empires** in the ancient world, specifically the civilizations of **Mesopotamia**, **Egypt**, **Greece**, and the Near East (**Assyria** and **Persia**).

The chapter begins with a definition of empire and the traits that separate it from other civilizations. Such traits include administrative practice, expanding communications and trade, and transmission of culture and ideas to conquered peoples. The author divides empire into two distinct types: **hegemony**, or rule by assent from the people, and **dominance**, or rule by military force. Included is a discussion concerning the probable causes of the decline and failure of empires which include: failure of leadership, over-extension of the administration, collapse of the economy, doubts over the ideology imposed by an empire, and military defeat of the empire by the combined forces of external enemies and/or colonized people in revolt.

Using the above discussion as a framework, this chapter recounts the histories of ancient empires by comparing and contrasting various features and results of their influence on various peoples and regions. The earliest empire begins with the Mesopotamian city-states who, through lack of unity, found themselves overrun and administrated under the **Akkadians**, led by the emperor **Sargon**. Through time, the region of the Near East witnessed the rise and fall of a number of empires, all of which competed with each other for control of the region, each with a varying degree of success and influence. These included the **Babylonian**, the **Hittite**, the **Assyrian**, the **Mitannis**, **Israelite**, and **Phoenician** empires.

The chapter continues with a lengthy discussion of the Egyptian empire and the reasons for its lengthy existence, centering around the geography of the region. The **Nile River** offered Egypt the means of centralizing its administration through reliable trade and communications. Egypt's period of empire ended with the **Nubian** conquest of Egypt's southern regions and the Assyrian subjugation of the northern regions. The advent of Assyrian rule and empire is developed as an example of dominance used to administer over conquered people.

The arrival of the Persians and the establishment of the Persian Empire signalled a new dominant force in majority of the Near East. The section offers a comparison/contrast of the administrative styles of **Cyrus II**, **Cambyses II**, and **Darius I**.

The final section of the chapter describes the origins of the Greeks and their road to empire. From the **Minoans** and **Myceneans**, to the rise of the Greek city-states, many of the images portrayed in the chapter are from the tales of **Homer** and **Herodotus**, which continue with the rise of the Greek military apparatus against the encroaching Persians. With the growing power of the city-states, and the declining threat from the Persians, the timing was right for a powerplay between the city-states, the most notable being the **Peloponnesian War** which pitted **Athens** against **Sparta**, resulting in a victory for the Spartans (with a little financial assistance from Persia). Though the Greeks of the Aegean peninsula were not unified, their contributions included the development of great art, literature, architecture, philosophy, and most importantly, the development of democracy by Solon (630 – 560 B.C.E.). The Greeks became unified under the conquests of Phillip and his son Alexander the Great, who spread Greek culture, language, and ideas throughout the known world.

Learning Objectives

After students have read and studied Chapter Five, they should be able to:

1. Define empire, be aware of the two forms of imperial rule, and how the two differ.
2. Describe the characteristics that form an empire.
3. List the causes of decline that occur in empires.
4. Compare and contrast the administrative styles of Cyrus II, Cambyses II, and Darius I.
5. Describe the development of the Greek city-states, how the Persian wars influenced the development of the Aegean peninsula, and ultimately caused the failure of the city-states to unite.
6. Describe the value system of early Greece and how it influenced their rise as a world power.
7. Analyze the ideology of Athenian democracy, and the reasons for its success in Greek culture.
8. Discuss the legacy of the empire that Alexander built, and how it influenced the rest of the known world.

Suggestions for Lecture Topics

1. In discussing the section on empire, explain why modern society still uses this term. Apply the often controversial term empire into modern language and compare and contrast the modern meaning of empire with the one applied to the ancient world.
2. Discuss the value, benefits, and possible disadvantages of empire. Though culture and ideas are exchanged, and the common good of history is served, point out the long dead cultures we may never know about due to the harsh and sometimes violent spread of other, more dominant cultures.
3. Discuss the traits that made a successful empire and why they would tend to work better than other, less successful, administrative practices. Use such examples as the Assyrians, Persians, Egyptians, and Greeks to describe commonalities and differences.
4. Discuss the impact of Greek culture on the known world. Point out the lasting quality of Greek influences that exist in the modern world. Discuss the reasons for these qualities having such a lasting impact on our modern culture.
5. Explain the development of Athenian democracy and how it differs from our modern definition of democracy. Point out the discussion made by Thucydides and Socrates in their interpretations of democracy.

Topics for Essays or Class Discussion

1. What is the specific quality that separates civilization from empire? What are some of the common traits shared by the empires in this chapter? Have empires existed in this century and do they still exist today? If so, give an example and a reason why you would define it as an empire.
2. Give some examples of what caused the decline in the following empires: Egypt, Assyria, and Persia. Do they share common traits in their failure to maintain an empire? If so, describe.
3. What are the traits or reasons for the failure of empires? Can you think of any modern (last 100 years) examples of empires failing due to one of the reasons listed in this chapter? If so, give at least one example and one reason why it failed.
4. Briefly describe the traits of Athenian democracy. Does our society reflect the same values of Greek democracy? How are they alike? How do they differ? Would you say that it is appropriate that U.S. society refers to itself as a democracy? Give at least one example or reason why you would or wouldn't.

Vocabulary

empire

Hammurabi

Indo-European

Herodotus

Socrates

democracy

Alexander

Plato

polis

deme

Agora

Solon

Aristotle

Phallocracy

Ecumene

Audio-Visual Resources

Athens and Ancient Greece: Great Cities of the Ancient World, 1994. **78 minutes, color.**

Reconstruction of 25 structures, including the Acropolis, the Parthenon, the Temple of Athena, the Agora, the Altar of the Twelve Gods, the Theater of Zeus, the Temple of Apollo at Delphi, and even a "re-creation" of the lost city of Atlantis.

Additional Text Resources

Maps:

The empire of Sargon (115)

Chapter Six: Rome and the Barbarians

Chapter Outline

A. The Extent and Legacy of the Roman Empire

    1. Extent

    2. Legacies of Rome

B. The Geographical Spread of Republic and Empire

    1. The conquest of Italy

    2. The conquest of Carthage and the western Mediterranean

    3. Expansion into southwestern Europe

    4. The conquest of the Greeks and the eastern Mediterranean

    5. The conquest of northwestern Europe: Gaul and Britain

    6. Completing the conquests: the empire at its zenith

    7. Political adjustments: from Republic to Empire

    8. Imperial Rome: How do we know?

C. The institution of the Empire

    1. Military power

    2. Political institutions

        a. patricians and plebeians

        b. Roman law

    3. Cultural policies and empire

        a. belied systems and religion

        b. Stoicism

        c. Christianity

        d. urban life

    4. Economic policies

D. The Effects of Empire on Rome

    1. Patriarchs, patrons, and clients

    2. Class and class conflict

    3. Urban splendor and squalor

    4. Gender relationships

    5. Attempts at reform

E. Rome's Ideology of Empire

F. The Barbarians and the Fall of Rome

    1. Who were the "Barbarians?"

        a. Celts

        b. Goths (Germans)

        c. Huns

    2. Barbarians: How do we know?

    3. The decline and fall of the Roman Empire

    4. Causes of the decline and fall

    5. Persistence of empire in the east: the Byzantine Empire

Chapter Summary

This chapter gives an account of the geographical expansion of the **Roman Republic** and **Empire**; it discusses the strengths and limits of the historical sources available for the study of Rome. It analyzes institutions of the empire (military, political, cultural, economic, and idealogical, and examines the class problems which undercut Rome's internal cohesion and strength. Included is a discussion of the rise of **Christianity** and its relationship to imperial rule. Finally, it discusses the invasions of "**barbarian**" peoples who attacked and eventually destroyed the empire.

The chapter begins by discussing the extent and legacy of the empire on the world. The Roman Empire encompassed the entire area surrounding the Mediterranean Sea and went as far north as **Great Britain**. The legacies of the Roman Empire--such as the **Latin** language, art and architecture, and how they have influenced other societies--are also discussed in this chapter. The chapter uses the example of the British, and how they tried to remake the world in the Roman image.

The chapter then moves on to discuss how the empire spread across the Mediterranean. It starts with the Roman conquest of **Italy** and how the Romans formed alliances with neighboring city-states. After covering the conquest of Italy, the chapter goes on to discuss the three **Punic Wars**, also known as the wars with **Carthage**, and their outcomes. The chapter continues with a discussion of the Roman conquest of **Spain**, **Gaul** (modern day France), and **Germania** (modern day Germany). Finally, it addresses the last two major areas conquered by Rome: Great Britain and **Egypt**.

The chapter then covers the major institutions and policies of the Empire: military, political, religious, cultural, and economic. The military was central to life in Rome. Its job was not only to protect, but also to conquer. When a town or area was taken over, the citizens of that town would be forced to send men, not gold, to the Roman army as tribute. The Romans used politics to placate those they conquered. The "**right of citizenship**" was used to entice nations to join the Roman Empire peacefully. Thus, Rome developed naturally into a conglomerate of many different cultures. As a different city or culture was conquered, aspects of the culture that the Romans found appealing would be appropriated into their own, thus altering Roman culture forever.

Although the Romans' main religion focused on the emperor as a god, there were many other religions present in the empire such as **Stoicism**, **Christianity**, and different forms of **paganism**. Initially, Christianity was considered as crime, but in 313 C.E., it was established as the main religion of the Roman Empire.

As Rome grew in power, it started to import goods from other countries. Because of Rome's desire to pay for these goods with metallic money (i.e. gold or silver), much of Rome's wealth left the empire.

In 476 C.E., the Roman Empire fell. For almost two hundred years prior to the fall, the empire had been under attack by hordes of barbarians. The three most prevalent groups of barbarians were the **Celts**, the **Goths**, and the **Huns**. These three repeatedly led attacks against Rome until its fall.

Learning Objectives

After students have read and studied Chapter Six, they should be able to:

1. Explain the legacy of the Roman Empire.
2. Locate on a world map the extent of the Roman Empire.

3. List the date of the three Punic Wars.
4. Discuss how Hannibal defeated the Romans in the Second Punic War.
5. Name the five major dynasties of the Roman Emperors.
6. Explain the origins of Stoicism.
7. List the three major groups of barbarians that attacked the Roman Empire
8. List the reasons for the decline and eventual fall of the Roman Empire.

Suggestions for Lecture Topics

1. Explain the importance that the three Punic Wars had on the development of the image of Rome as a great power. Discuss the importance of the destruction of Carthage after the Third Punic War.
2. Discuss the importance of Stoicism, Christianity, and the emperor-god forms of religion upon the people of the Roman Empire.
3. Discuss the impact of the barbarian invasions upon the Roman Empire.
4. Explain why the Eastern Empire was able to outlast the Western Empire.

Topics for Essays or Class Discussion

1. How does Rome's military policy of "New Wisdom" work? Discuss examples of how this policy might be utilized.
2. In what ways has Roman society influenced modern society?
3. Compare and contrast the Roman ideal of equality between the sexes and the reality of the treatment of both sexes.

Vocabulary

Punic Wars
Gaul
Pax Romana
praetors
latifundia
Caesar

Hannibal
Alexander the Great
consuls
tribunes
Augustus Caesar
plebeians

Audio-Visual Resources

Great Cities of the Ancient World: **1993. 60 minutes, color.**

The grandeur of Imperial Rome and Pompeii is reconstructed by archaeologists, historians, and video artists.

Additional Text Resources

Maps:

The Roman Empire (150)

Eurasian Trade (171)

The coming of the Barbarians (179)

Rome's successors (180)

The Byzantine Empire (182)

Document Extracts:

Rome's Code of Laws: Two Contrasting Perspectives (165)

Features:

Spotlight:

Chapter Seven: China

Chapter Outline

A. Introduction: the Qin, Han, Sui, and Tang Dynasties

B. The Chinese Empire: <u>How do we know?</u>

    1. Confucian texts

    2. Daoist and legalist writings

    3. Histories

    4. Archaeology: gravesites, tombs, inscriptions

C. The Qin Dynasty: <u>What do we know?</u>

    1. Military power and mobilization

    2. Economic power

    3. Administrative power

    4. The fall of the Qin Dynasty

D. Ideologies of Empire

    1. Qin Shi Huangdi

    2. Han Feizi and Legalism

    3. Laozi and Daoism

    4. Confucianism

    5. Qin Shi Huangdi, the Legalists and the Confucianists

E. The Han Dynasty

    1. Confucian influence

    2. Humility and women

    3. Military power

    4. Economic power

    5. Administrative power

F. The "Three Kingdoms and Six Dynasties" Period

G. Reunification Under the Sui and Tang Dynasties

    1. Achievement of the Sui: the Grand Canal

    2. Achievements of the Tang

H. Greater China

    1. Processes of assimilation

    2. The north and northwest

    3. The south and southeast

    4. Vietnam

    5. Korea

    6. Japan

I. China and Rome: Differences and Similarities

    1. Differences

    2. Similarities

Chapter Summary

This chapter discusses the Chinese Empire during its first 1100 years, from 221 B.C.E. to 907 C.E. The fractures and unifications of the **Qin**, **Han**, **Sui**, and **Tang Dynasties** are broken down and described in a thorough manner within this chapter.

The chapter begins with a consideration of the sources of information on this time period in China, and the question is asked, "How do we know?" China prepared and transmitted the most fully and continously documented history of any ancient empire.

The main historical sources for early Chinese history (551 – 479 B.C.E.) are a series of written texts by **Confucius**. **Daoism** and **Legalism** also produced major literary works of this time period.

The Qin Dynasty, the first in China's history, lasted for over two-and-a-half centuries (481 – 221 B.C.E.). Enormous public works projects were undertaken during this dynasty for the purpose of public safety and economic productivity. The **Great Wall** was built, along with vast irrigation systems and canals.

China's historical records were written and preserved by a philosophical elite. This was the reason for China's profound concern with the philosophy and ideology of its empire. The Qin Dynasty was influenced by Legalism, which was the belief that strictly enforced laws were the best assurance of a good and stable government. Daoism and Confucianism were two other major schools of political and ethical thought. Daoism, a more mystical school, was rarely applied to government, but was often a source of comfort to public men in their private lives. Confucianism, on the other hand, was more didactic in its approach to government in its belief that good government depended on good officials, benevolence, virture, and culture.

A new dynasty formed when the Qin Dynasty fell. This was the Confucian-oriented Han Dynasty, which began its rule in about 206 B.C.E. The new emperor of this dynasty, **Liu Bang**, completely immersed himself in Confucianism by surrounding himself with men educated in Confucian principles. During this time period, a new social and political hierarchy emerged, with scholars at the top, followed by farmers, artisans, and merchants. The influence of Confucianism appeared in four other areas. First, history became more important than ever. Second, the Han ruler **Wudi** established an elite imperial academy to teach specially selected scholar-bureaucrats the wisdom of Confucius. Third, an imperial conference of Confucian legal scholars was convened to codify and establish the principles for applying case law, ultimately establishing the Chinese legal system for years to come. Finally, Confucian scholars began to establish principles of conduct for women. The Confucian concept of the woman's role in society was one of a housewife, nurturer, and provider of support for China's men.

When the Han Dynasty fell, China divided into three states: the **Wei**, **Wu**, and **Shu**. Reuniting the empire required the restoration of military, economic, and administrative power. The Sui Dynasty provided all three and rose to power. Eventually, even the Sui fell and was succeeded by the Tang Dynasty. Apart from three periods totalling 133 years, the Chinese Empire has stood united for more than fourteen centuries.

Learning Objectives

After students have read and studied Chapter Seven, they should be able to:

1. Name the four Chinese dynasties.
2. Define Legalism and know its influence on the Qin Dynasty.
3. Define Daoism and know what its role was in Chinese politics.
4. Define Confucianism and know its effect on Chinese culture.
5. Describe the public works projects that contributed to Chinese culture during the Qin Dynasty.
6. Trace the roles of women in China's history, noting changes in the perception of them between dynasties.
7. Explain the specific role of women in Chinese society during the Han Dynasty.
8. Discuss the transition between the "Three Kingdoms" period and the reunification period, describing the factors that led to reunification.

Suggestions for Lecture Topics

1. In discussing the sources that recount Chinese history, introduce the term "bias" and what it means. Let students know that while pondering the meaning of a document, they have to consider where it came from and who its author was.
2. Explain the role Kong Fizi, Confucius, played in Chinese culture and politics.
3. Discuss the role of propaganda and its use by Chinese rulers through the centuries to control the population.
4. How was Daoism a great influence on Chinese politics, even though it wasn't directly applicable to government?

Topics for Essays or Class Discussion

1. What was the role of women in Chinese society? How has it changed through the centuries?
2. Confucianism influenced Chinese society greatly. How did it influence government and what were the four other areas it affected?
3. Describe the public works projects which were undertaken during the Qin Dynasty and what purposes they served for Chinese citizens.
4. Discuss the roles of Legalism and Daoism in Chinese politics.

Vocabulary

Daoism	scholar
Legalism	reunification
Confucianism	bias
Buddhism	Qin
dynasty	Han
assimilation	Sui
feudal system	Tang
ideology	hierarchy
bureaucrats	

Audio-Visual Resources

The Great Wall of China; produced and directed by Patrick Fleming. New York: Ambrose Video, 1995. 26 minutes, 29 seconds (VHS).

Chin, China's first Emperor and namesake, created a nation whose boundaries have remained unchanged for almost two thousand years. The Great Wall of China, arguably the world's most impressive architectual work, was built during Chin's reign. This video outlines the construction of this great work and describes the reasons for its creation.

Additional Text Resources

Maps:

Classical China (197)

Chinese expansion (198)

The Tang revival (207)

Chinese technology (209)

Asian imperial capitals (Chang'an and Nara) (214)

Document Extracts:

Selections from *The Analects* of Confucius (195)

Spotlight:

A Han Dynasty Code of Conduct (200)

Chapter Eight: Indian Empires

Chapter Outline

A. Cultural Cohesion in a Divided Subcontinent

B. Settlement in South Asia

    1. Aryan settlement

    2. The Maurya Dynasty

    3. Asoka

C. Familial, Social, Economic, and Religious Institutions

D. The Indian Empire: <u>How do we know?</u>

    1. Archaeology and philology

    2. Written texts

        a. the Puranas

        b. the Vedas

        c. the Bramanas and the Upanishads

        d. the *Mahabharata* and the *Ramayana*

        e. the *Bhagavadgita*

        f. the *Artha-sastra*

E. Statecraft under the Mauryas and Guptas: <u>What do we know?</u>

    1. the Mauryan Empire

    2. the Gupta Empire

F. Huna Invasions and the End of the North Indian Empire

    1. Origins of the Xiongu

    2. Legacies of the Hunas

G. Regional Diversity and Power

H. Sea Trade and Cultural Influence: from Rome to Southeast Asia

    1. Tamil culture in southeas India

    2. Southeast Asia: "Greater India"

I. India, China, and Rome: Empires and Intermediate Institutions

Chapter Summary

This chapter relates to the initial settlement and development of what is now the subcontinent of **India**. Bordered by mountains to the north, and oceans to the east, south, and west, India's natural boundaries would invariably influence one cohesive state. However, from the years 2500 B.C.E. until India's independence in 1947, there were many takeovers by a number of different clans and dynasties. The main theme of this chapter is to explain how cultural stability was achieved despite numerous political and religious changes which occurred on a regular basis.

India was established around 2500 B.C.E. by groups of settlers who had made their way across the **Himalayas** and across the seas. These groups were called **Janapadas** with each group settling in a different area of the Indian subcontinent. A rivalry between the groups evolved resulting in continuous skirmishes for land and natural resources. No one group was able to gain enough control to form any kind of alliance, so these battles continued.

Nevertheless, a common culture--one influenced by both **Buddhism** as well as the **caste** system already in place among the different Janapandas-- began to take shape amid all of this political conflict.

The first part of the chapter attempts to explain how a common culture could possibly arise from such politically different groups. The answer has to do mostly with the bonding religion of Buddhism.

The chapter then delves into the two great empires that arose from these Janapadas, or diverse groups. The first dynasty, the **Mauryan Empire**, came to prominence in 324 B.C.E. and flourished until 185 B.C.E. Its rule was based on the principle of having a strong central government that maintained tight control over its citizens. The Mauryan's first emperor, **Chandragupta Maurya**, ruled from 321 – 297 B.C.E., and forged alliances with those communities that surrounded those nearest to him. This strategy was quite effective when the Maurya would wage war against their neighbors, as this would invariably lead his enemies into fighting an unwinnable two-front war. This strategy enabled the Mauryan Empire to expand over most of Northern India. Another prominent leader was **Asoka** (273 – 232 B.C.E.) who instituted Buddhism as the state religion in 250 B.C.E., and brought peace to a militarian empire. However, the empire fell in 185 B.C.E., just 45 years after his death.

For the next 500 years, India reverted to a group of warring tribes that held several different parts of the subcontinent. This lack of cohesion left the region vulnerable to attacks from outside forces which included many Asian and Indo-Greek groups.

The next group to occupy a central role in the unification of India was the **Guptas**, who ruled for about 200 years. Their political system differed from the Mauryan in the fact that they would request only money from those communities they conquered. Their rule was less strict and greatly appreciated by the conquered groups they ruled over.

The chapter concludes with a comparison of the Roman, Chinese, and Indian empires. While it is difficult to compare the three, the chapter manages to compare and contrast three very different empires and make connections that are accurate and prudent to the chapter.

Learning Objectives

After students have read and studied Chapter Eight, they should be able to:

1. Explain the accomplishments of Asoka in the Mauryan Empire.
2. State when India was settled.
3. Describe the natural boundaries surrounding India.
4. Construct a map of India depicting the extent of the two empires.
5. Describe India's movement from Buddhism to Hinduism.
6. Define the Janapadas and Maha-Janapadas.
7. Explain the significance of Asoka's seven pillar edicts.
8. Compare and contrast the Mauryan Empire to the Gupta Empire.
9. Explain how religion played an important role in the social and political structures of ancient India.
10. Discuss the effects of international trade with Europe on Indian civilizations.
11. Explain the fall of the North Indian Empire.

Suggestions for Lecture Topics

1. Discuss the settlement of India and why the area was so divided when, geographically, it was very homogeneous and set apart from the rest of the world by its natural boundaries. Also include a discussion on why the cultures of the different Janapadas was cohesive while their political views were so different.
2. Present the Mauryan Empire and explain its significance in Indian history. Explain how it was the first great empire and that it unified a major part of India under one set of laws, or the Artha-Sastra. Also include a discussion about the great leaders of this empire (Chandragupta and Asoka). Also incorporate the significance of the caste system in this dynasty.
3. Discuss the Gupta Empire and explain how it came to power. What were the differences between the Guptas and the Mauryans? How did Chandra Gupta II come into power and explain his method of rule as compared to the Mauryans. Investigate the legacy of the Guptas (i.e. the resurgence of Hinduism and the use of Sanskrit).
4. Discuss the effects of the Huna invasions of India in the years 460 C.E. and 500 C.E.
5. Compare and contrast the empires of China, Rome, and India.

Topics for Essays or Class Discussion

1. Explain how the Indian culture was cohesive while the subcontinent itself was divided.
2. Decide which empire, the Mauryan or the Gupta, was more effective in unifying India. State reasons for your choice; include political and social policies or ideals.
3. Why was there a resurgence of the Hindu religion after Buddhism had been a mainstay for 550 years?
4. If you could live in India during any time period mentioned in this chapter, which one would you choose and why?

Vocabulary

Indus Civilization	Janapadas
Maha-Janapadas	Mauryan Dynasty
Gupta Dynasty	Asoka Maurya
Ganges River Valley	Puranas
Veda	Artha-Sastra
caste	Sanskrit
Hunas	Buddhism
Hinduism	

Audio-Visual Resources

The World History Videodisc: **1991. 45 minutes, color.**

This gives an overview of the history of India from ancient times to the present, focusing on several of the topics in this chapter.

Additional Text Resources

Maps:

Mauryan India (227)

Gupta India (233)

Classical South Asia (236)

Document Extracts:

The Asoka Pillar and Rock Inscriptions (229)

Tamil Culture in Southeast India (237)

Spotlight:

Gandharan Art (230)

Chapter Nine: Hinduism and Buddhism

Chapter Outline

A. The Historian and Religious Belief: <u>How do we know?</u>

B. Hinduism

    1. The origins of Hinduism: <u>How do we know?</u>

    2. Sacred geography and pilgrimage

    3. The central beliefs of Hinduism

        a. the *Rigveda*

            i. Purusha and the caste system

            ii. *varna* and *jati*

        b. the *Bramanas* and the *Upanishads*

            i. *brahman* and *atman*

            ii. *samsara* and *moksha*

            iii. *dharma* and *karma*

        c. the *Puranas*

    4. *Bhakti*: the path of mystical devotion

    5. Temples and shrines

    6. Religion and rule

    7. Hinduism and Southeast Asia

        a. <u>How do we know?</u>

        b. Hinduism and Buddhism in Southeast Asia

C. Buddhism

    1. Siddartha Guatama: the Buddha

        a. Mythistory: <u>How do we know?</u>

        b. the "Four Noble Truths," and the "Noble Eightfold Path"

        c. the Sangha and the doctrine

        d. Theravada and Mahayana Buddhism

    2. The decline of Buddhism in India

    3. Jainism

    4. Buddhism in China and Japan

        a. arrival in China: the Silk Route

        b. Buddhism under the Tang Dynasty

        c. Buddhism in Japan

            i. Buddhism's arrival in Japan

            ii. Japanese Buddhist sects

    5. Images of the Buddha

D. Hinduism and Buddhism: a Comparison

Chapter Summary

Chapter Nine discusses **Hinduism** and **Buddhism** from a definition to the history of both. The first part of the chapter explains the definition of religion and early religious practices, then continues with a discussion of the five different manifestations and effects on religious beliefs–the manifestation of time, space, language and literature, artistic and cultural creativity, and the creation of a religious organization.

The chapter then goes on to the origins of Hinduism. It is the result of a weaving together of many diverse and ancient traditions of India that began before recorded history. Although many scholars believed, until recently, that Hinduism began with the **Aryan** invasions of 1700 – 1200 B.C.E., archaeological digs have unearthed evidence that many of the same beliefs were practiced long before these invasions. What the Aryan invasions contributed to Hinduism was the preservation of its traditions in **Sanskrit**, the written language of the Aryans.

What makes Hinduism unique among all of the world religions is that almost all Hindus come from India, or are from Indian descent. This is made clear by its sacred geography and places of pilgrimage for Hindus–all are in India, including **Somnath** (on the far west coast), **Hardwar** and **Rishikesh** (in the far north), and **Kanya Kumari** (at the southern tip). What all these holy cities have in common are religious shrines and statues of gods.

The chapter covers the central beliefs of Hinduism, which are far less rigid and dogmatic than other religions. Hinduism is a living, changing system of beliefs and practices that has, over time, remained flexible and accomodating to the introduction of new texts to the Hindu legacy.

The sacred writings of Hinduism consist of four scriptures, or **vedas**. The **Rigveda**, composed between about 1500 and 1200 B.C.E. by **Brahmin** priests, is the most venerated of the veda, consisting of a collection of 1,028 verses set down in Sanskrit covering a broad range of topics from the creation of the world to the significance of life in this world. It also introduces the mythic origin of the **caste** system–the belief that a mythical creature named **Pursha** was carved into four sections, each of which symbolized one of the principal divisions of the caste system. The caste system was considered hereditary, the blood and semen of one group could not mix with another's. Dietary laws also differed between the castes, the Brahmin priests were required to be vegetarian, while the **Kshatriya** warrior class could eat only meat. Today the caste system has expanded to tens of thousands of castes, many of which lay claim to the same status–there may be hundreds of different castes that claim to be Brahmins. The other three scriptures are the **Yajurveda**, consisting of prayers and sacrificial formulas, the **Samaveda**, consisting of religious tunes and chants, and the **Atharva-veda**, used primarily by the **Atharvans**--priests who officiate at sacrifices.

Unlike the major monotheistic religions, Hinduism has a pantheon of over 1,000 gods, each having its own different qualities. Two major gods are **Shiva**, the god of destruction, and **Vishnu**, the preserver. The main god for the Brahmins is **Brahma**, the creator god who, with his four arms and heads, symbolizes the four **vedas**, **castes**, and **yugas** (ages of the world). The Brahmins even had their own religious literature called the **Brahamanas**–a set of instructions on ritual and sacrifice.

The **Bhagavadgita** is discussed in the next part of the chapter, along with poems that discuss this Hindu scripture (the **Ramayana** and the **Mahabharata**), which summarizes the main elements of Hindu belief, as well as pointing the way to spiritual fulfillment. The **Puranas**, on the other hand, are eighteen major and eighteen minor collections of folk tales which recount legends of gods, kings, and the creation and destruction of the universe. A new, mystical aspect of Hinduism began to emerge in around 500 C.E. The **Bhakti**, while based on classical texts such as the **Gita**, is perhaps the most subversive of these writings, as it revolted against hierarchy in religion and specifically, the power of the Brahmin priesthood.

The chapter continues with coverage of the holy temples and shrines of Hindus, including the **Kailasanatha Temple** at Ellora. This temple, an ancient pilgrimage center not only for Hindus, but for **Jains** and Buddhists as well, was carved into volcanic stone sometime between 757 and 790 C.E. Another major religious shrine for Hindus is the **Kandariya Mahadeo Temple** at Khajuraho, built between 1025 and 1050 C.E. This shrine consists of towers and sculptures dramatizing human and divine activity, which often includes sexually explicit depictions--attributed to **Tantric** sects of Hinduism.

While Hinduism rarely seeked converts outside of India, it still managed to move eastward to **Southeast Asia**. The spread of Hinduism into Southeast Asia was due mainly to politics–the powers of the Hindu temple and the

Brahmin priesthood were imported to validate royal authority in this region. Buddhist monks, as well as the Brahmin priests, were invited to establish and consolidate power in Southeast Asia. This inextricably ties Hinduism and Buddhism together in the region. While Hinduism died out in Southeast Asia by the fourteenth century, Buddhism continues to thrive. The opposite is true for the Indian subcontinent, where Buddhism is all but extinct from the land where it originated, and Hinduism flourishes.

Buddhism, like Hinduism, arose out of India, emphasizing the spiritual over the earthly, and speculating on the existence of other worlds. Rather than being an amalgamation of various cultures and beliefs in the subcontinent, Buddhism had a single founder, a set of originating scriptures, and an order of monks. Buddhim renounced the caste system and spread through Southeast Asia in such areas as **Myanmar**, **Thailand**, **Cambodia**, **Laos**, and **Vietnam**, where, unlike Hinduism, it remains to this day. In addition, it won over many converts in the far eastern areas of **China**, **Korea** and **Japan**.

The chapter continues with a discussion of Buddhism's founding father, **Siddartha Gautama**, or **Buddha**. Born in 563 B.C.E. to a father who belonged to the kshatriya warrior class, Siddartha left his family behind at the age of twenty-nine to find an "antidote to sorrow," and to teach this to others. Upon reaching **enlightenment**, where he determined that personal desire and passion were the cause of human suffering, he set forth his **Four Noble Truths**, and the **Noble Eightfold Path** to emancipate humanity from its own passions, and subsequently, from suffering. The truths consisted of the noble truth of **Sorrow**, the noble truth of **Arising from Sorrow**, the noble truth of the **Stopping of Sorrow**, and the noble truth of the **Way Which Leads to the Stopping of Sorrow**. The Noble Eightfold Path consisted of Right Views, Right Resolve, Right Speech, Right Conduct, Right Livelihood, Right Effort, Right Recollection, and Right Meditation.

The **Sangha** was an order of monks that followed the teachings of Buddha. Open to all men (and for a time, women) regardless of their caste, they were noted for their shaved heads, saffron robes, and vow of celibacy. Despite their adherence to Buddha's teachings, they were allowed to think and act freely. After Buddha's death in 483 B.C.E., the Sangha orchestrated a series of meetings to codify his teachings. The third of these conventions, held at Pataliputra in Asoka, revealed a split among the attendants over whether Buddha was a god or a human. The fourth council, held sometime in the first century C.E. in **Kashmir**, revealed an even greater discord among the Buddhists. The **Theravada** Buddhists had become the prevailing form of Buddhism in most of Southeast Asia, but a sect that had been growing for over two centuries, the **Mahayana** sect of Buddhism, posed a serious challenge to the status quo.

The adherents of Mahayana Buddhism believed in religious merit which could be achieved by the performance of good deeds. They also embellished on the concept of nirvana, designating it as a heavenly afterlife, and perceived Buddha to have transcended his human state to become a messiah-like figure, who presided over this Mahayana heaven. Buddha was no longer just a human, but now existed in three forms: **Amitabha**, the Buddha in heaven, **Gautama**, the historical Buddha on earth, and **Avalokiteshvara**, the freely moving spirit.

Buddhism began to decline in the Indian subcontinent when regional rulers began to side with the Brahmin priests rather than the Buddhists monks. Mahayana Buddhism had become so similar to Hinduism that there seemed little need to maintain any distinction. Ostensibly, Hinduism became attractive to less strict adherents of Buddhism because, in its ever-evolving state, it had grown to encompass Buddhism–one could worship the Buddha within the context of Hinduism, for he was often viewed as being an incarnation of Vishnu. Ultimately, the end of Buddhism in India came with the Muslim invasions of the region, occurring between 1000 and 1200 C.E. Already in a weakened state, Buddhism was unable to put up much resistance and was all but eradicated from the subcontinent.

Despite its misfortune in India, Buddhism remained a force in Southeast Asia and, in fact, spread to the far east with relative ease, due in part to the **Silk Route**, a pathway from India to China that was invariably used for the communication and the silk trade. Taking firm root in China after the fall of the Han dynasty in 220 C.E., Buddhism did not face overwhelming opposition from the native Daoists because, despite their initial rivalry, the mystical aspects of Mahayan Buddhism appealed to them. Ultimately, the two faiths validated each other–Daoists saw Buddha as a manifestation of **Lao Zi** during his travels in India, while Buddhists accorded the status of **bodhisattva** (a person who has achieved great moral and spiritual wisdom) to both Lao Zi and **Confucius**.

Buddhism first arrived in Japan in 552 C.E. from **Korea** in the form of texts and statues from a **Paekchean** king asking for help in a war against **Silla**, another Korean kingdom. Half a century later, **Prince Shotoku Taishi** (573 C.E. – 621 C.E.) helped Buddhism gain widespread acceptance by building numerous temples and shrines, including the **Horyuji**, in the city of Nara. Always interested in learning more about Buddhism, he often invited Korean Buddhist clergy to Japan and would dispatch missions to Sui China in order to centralize his political rule.

In 604 C.E., Buddhism was officially included in Shotoku's constitution. By the twelfth century, Japan entered its Buddhist Age.

Learning Objectives

After students have read and studied Chapter Nine, they should be able to:

1. Discuss the origin and growth of Hinduism.
2. Discuss the origin and growth of Buddhism.
3. Locate on a map two of the sacred cities of Hinduism–Kanya Kumari, and Somnath.
4. List the major Hindu gods and what they symbolize.
5. Name the five sacred writings of the Hindus.
6. Explain the four noble truths as told by Buddha.
7. Explain the four sacred writings of Buddhism
8. Discuss Buddhism under the Tang Dynasty.
9. Trace the history of both Hinduism and Buddhism from 300 B.C.E. to 1200 C.E.
10. Explain the poem *The Transience of Life* written from a woman's perspective.

Suggestions for Lecture Topics

1. Explain the eight major gods of Hinduism and stress the importance and significance of each.
2. Point out and explain how Buddhism migrated from India to China, and subsequently to Japan and Korea. Also, explain the routes taken and other ways the religion could have been spread.
3. Explain the five sacred writings and their significance to the Hindu religion.
4. Discuss the life, times, and death of Buddha. Explain why he is so significant to Buddhists.
5. Explain the positive and negative effects of believing in many gods.
6. Discuss Buddhism and Hinduism as each evolved in Southeast Asia.

Topics for Essays or Class Discussion

1. What specific characteristics do Buddhists and Hindus share? Are there any major differences between the two? If so, what are they?
2. How did Buddhism get from India to Japan?
3. Explain Buddha's four noble truths and their significance.
4. Discuss Buddha's teachings and why they are so important to Buddhists.

Vocabulary

Sanskrit	amalgam
Brahmin priest	Kshatriya warriors
caste system	Ashwamedha
Atman	Bhagavadgita
Stupas	Caityas

Audio-Visual Resources

The Principles and Practices of Zen: 1992. 116 minutes, color.

This movie is about Buddhists and what they practice and preach, describing the principles they follow, as well as what they believe in and what will happen to them in the afterlife.

Additional Text Resources

Maps:

Document Extracts:

Features:

Spotlight:

Chapter 10 - Judaism and Christianity

Chapter Outline

A. Judaism

    1. The Covenant and monotheism

    2. Early Judaism: <u>How do we know?</u> (the TaNaKh or Old Testament)

    3. Essential beliefs of Judaism in early scriptures

        a. a single, all-powerful God

        b. a divinely chosen people and a "promised land"

        c. a divinely ordained law code: the Ten Commandments

        d. the Jewish calendar

    4. The Evolution of God

    5. Later Books of the Jewish Scripture

        a. the teachings of the Prophets: morality and hope

        b. gender relations

    6. Defeat, Exile, and Redefinition

        a. the Assyrian and Babylonian exiles

        b. the Jewish Revolt and the diaspora

    7. Minority-majority relations in the diaspora

    8. Christianity emerges from Judaism

B. Christianity

    1. Mythistory: <u>How do we know?</u>

    2. Jesus's life, teachings, and disciples

        a. the story in the Gospels

        b. Judaea in Jesus's time

        c. new rituals and teachings

        d. Jesus and the Jewish establishment

        e. miracle and mystery: passion and resurrection

    3. Christianity organizes

        a. the early disciples

        b. Paul organizes the early church

        c. adaptations of other philosophies and rituals

        d. the Christian calendar

        e. gender relations in Christianity

        f. slavery

        g. struggle for survival in Rome

4. Christianity triumphant

    a. the conversion of Constantine

    b. how had Christianity succeeded?

5. Doctrine: definition and dispute

    a. Augustine and Neoplatonism

    b. original sin, sexuality, and salvation

    c. church dogma: discipline and battles

        i. the Council of Nicaea

        ii. persecution of dissidents

6. Official Christianity in the wake of empire

    a. conversion of the barbarians

    b. monasteries and missionaries

    c. the Church: east and west

        i. icons and iconoclasm

        ii. the Great Schism

    d. Christianity in Western Europe: the Papacy

    e. Charlemagne

Chapter Summary

The story of **Judaism** begins some 3800 years ago with one man's vision of a single, unique God of all creation. God and **Abraham** sealed a covenant stating that Abraham's descendants would forever revere and worship that God, and God, in turn, would forever watch over and protect them. From then until now Judaism has remained a relatively small, family-based religion, focused in part in the land promised by God to Abraham, **Israel**, with branches throughout the world.

The Jewish belief in one god, **monotheism**, was not simply a reduction in the number of gods from many to one. In contrast with paganism's many gods of diverse temperaments, the new monotheism provided a much more definitive statement of right and wrong. At the same time demanded much greater conformity in both faith and action, calling for adherence to a strict code of ethics within a community governed by laws proclaimed by God.

Although the number of Jews has always been small, many of Judaism's core beliefs were later incorporated into **Christianity** and **Islam**, the two great monotheistic faiths that have come to include half the world's population today.

Our knowledge of early Jewish history comes from the scriptures known collectively as the **TaNaKh**. The narratives of the five books of the **Torah** abound with miracles, as God intervenes continuously in the history of the Jews. The Torah remains one of the greatest examples of mythistory. Its stories are not necessarily literal, historical records, but their version of events gave birth to the Jewish people's concept of itself and helped to define its character and principal beliefs.

Jewish religious leaders reconstituted earlier pagan nature celebrations into a calendar of national religious celebration. For example, a spring festival of renewal was incorporated into **Passover**, the commemoration of the exodus from Egypt.

Jews represent both an ethnic community and universal religion. This dual identity became especially clear as Jews were exiled by foreign conquest out of the land of Israel as part of a plan to encourage their assimilation and to open up the land of Israel to foreign immigration.

Jews were driven out of their promised land into exile several times: by the **Assyrians** in 721 B.C.E., and following, anti-imperial revolts, by the **Romans** in 135 C.E. In addition, many Jews traveled willingly, by free choice, throughout the trade and cultural networks that had been established by the **Persians** in the sixth century B.C.E., extended by **Alexander the Great** in the fourth century B.C.E., and perpetuated by the Roman Empire. The Roman exile of 135 C.E., however, fundamentally and permanently altered Jewish existence. It removed all but a few Jews from their political homeland until the twentieth century.

In general, Jews remained socially and religiously distinct wherever they traveled. This identification was imposed partially from the outside by others, partially by internal discipline and loyalty to the group, its traditions, and laws. Jewish history becomes a case study also of tolerance and intolerance of minorities by majority peoples around the world.

Jesus Christ, the founder of Christianity, was born to an unmarried Jewish woman and her carpenter fiancé in a manger in **Bethlehem**, 10 miles (16 kilometers) from **Jerusalem**, some 2000 years ago. Jesus grew into an astonishingly powerful preacher, who promised eternal life and happiness to the simple, poor and downtrodden people of colonial Judea if only they would keep their faith in God. As Jesus' fame spread, the Jewish religious authorities and the Roman colonial administrators feared his attacks on their establishments. To prevent any potential rebellion, the Roman government crucified him when he was thirty-three years old.

But death did not stop Jesus' message. His disciples, and especially **Paul**, newcomer to the faith who was converted through a miraculous encounter with the dead Jesus, took his message of compassion, salvation, and eternal life to Rome. Despite early persecution, Christianity increased in influence, until it became the official religion of the empire. Spread through the networks of the empire, it ultimately became the most important organizing force in post-Roman Europe. The message of compassion and exultation and the organization of the church expanded throughout the different churches and denominations, declaring themselves followers of this son of God, the simple preacher from Judea.

Helena, the mother of the Emperor **Constantine** (r. 306 – 337 C.E.), had churches built in Asia Minor and the Holy Land and traveled to Jerusalem, seeking the cross on which Jesus died. In 313C.E., Constantine himself had a vision in which a cross with the words *in hoc signo vinces* (in this sign you will be victorious) appeared to him the night before he won the critical battle that made him sole emperor in the Western Empire. He immediately declared Christianity legal throughout the Roman Empire.

Constantine sponsored the **Council of Nicea** in 325 C.E., the largest assembly of bishops of local churches up to that time. He convened the Council primarily to establish the central theological doctrines of Christianity, but it also established a church organization for the Roman Empire.

In 399 C.E., the Emperor **Theodosius** (r. 379 – 395 C.E.) declared Christianity the official religion of the Roman Empire. He outlawed paganism and severely restricted Judaism, initiating centuries of bitter Christian persecution of both traditions.

As it grew after receiving official recognition, the Roman Church refined its theology. The most influential theologian of the period, **Augustine** (354 – 430 C.E.), **Bishop of Hippo** in north Africa, wrote *The City of God* to explain Christianity's relationship to competing religions and philosophies, and to the Roman government with which it was increasingly intertwined.

Some theological disputes led to violence, especially as the church attempted to suppress doctrinal disagreement. The most divisive concerned the nature of the divinity; God and the father, wholly transcendent, was more sacred than the son who had walked the earth. The Council of Nicea, which was convened in 325 C.E. to resolve this dispute, issued an official statement of creed affirming Jesus' complete divinity and his indivisibility from God.

Christianity spread to western and northern Europe along the communication and transportation networks of the Roman Empire. As the empire weakened and dissolved, Christianity remained and flourished.

Today, **Eastern Orthodoxy** and **Roman Catholicism** share the same fundamental faith and scripture and they maintain official communication with each other, but they developed many history differences over church organization, authority, aesthetics, and language.

As in the West, monastic life flourished in the **Byzantine Empire**. The greatest missionary activity of the Eastern monks come later than in the West. Hemmed in by the Roman Empire and the barbarians to the West and by the growing power of Islam to the east after about 650 C.E., Byzantium turned its missionary efforts northward, toward Russia.

In other regions of east-central Europe, Rome and Byzantium competed in spreading their religious and cultural messages and organizations. In the **Great Schism** of 1054 C.E., the two churches were definitively split into two sects, the Latin (or Roman Catholic) Church–predominant in Western Europe–and the Greek Orthodox Church, which prevailed in the east.

In the Byzantine Empire, the state became, in effect, an armed force. In Rome, the pope felt surrounded by the hostile powers of **Constantinople** and Islam to the east and south, and several **Gothic** kings to the north and west. Seeking alliances with strongmen, he turned to a Frank **Charles (Carolus) Martel**, who gave his name to the **Carolingian** family. Martel had pushed the Muslims out of France in 732 C.E., and in 754 C.E., his son Pepin III answered the call of Pope Stephan II for help in fighting the Lombard Goths, who were invading Italy and threatening the papal possessions.

Pepin III's son Charles ruled as **Charles the Great (Charlemagne)** and was crowned Roman Emperor by **Pope Leo III** on Christmas Day, 800 C.E., in Rome. Emperor and Pope had agreed to attempt to reconstruct the historic Roman Empire, and to achieve this goal Charlemagne spent all his adult lifetime in warfare, continuing the military expeditions of his father and grandfather.

The Carolingian family remained powerful until about the end of the century, but then could no longer fight off the new invasions of the western Christian world by **Magyars**, **Norsemen**, and **Arabs**. In this era, 600 – 1100 C.E., the church rather than any overtly political organization, gave Europe its fundamental character and order. The Magyar and Norse invaders, like the Germans before them, converted to Catholicism. By the end of the eleventh century, the Roman Catholic church, as well as the political authorities of western Europe, was preparing to confront Islam.

Learning Objectives

After students have read and studied Chapter Ten, they should be able to:

1. Know that many of Judaism's core beliefs were later incorporated into Christianity and Islam.
2. Summarize the important events in the life of Jesus Christ.
3. Be able to describe the development of Christianity from a small sect to a major world religion.
4. Understand that while Eastern Orthodoxy and Roman Catholicism share the same faith and scripture, they developed many differences over church, organization, authority, aesthetics, and language.

Suggestions for Lecture Topics

1. Discuss why Jesus represents both an ethnic community and a universal religion.
2. Explain why Paul is regarded as the second founder of Christianity.
3. Discuss the strengths and weaknesses of the Roman Empire. Explain the unified Roman Empire's affect on the spread of Christianity.
4. List and explain the factors which can effect the decline of a great power.

Topics for Essays or Class Discussion

1. Explain the basic message of Jesus to his contemporaries. Discuss the major tenets of Christianity.
2. Discuss the role of the monasteries on converting and disciplining the barbarians.
3. Explain how Christianity spread despite persecution.
4. Describe how Christian teachings are rooted in Jewish traditions.

Vocabulary

monotheism

Judaism

Pharaoh Akhenaton

Torah

Jesus Christ

Augustine of Hippo

Arius

Venerable Bede

Charles (Carolus) Martel

Emperor Constantine

Council of Nicea

Emperor Theodosius

The City of God

Eastern Orthodoxy

Byzantine Empire

Charlemagne

Audio-Visual Resources

Early Christianity and the Rise of the Church: 1989. 2 parts, 30 minutes each, color.

One of the series, The Western Tradition; studies the growth and development of early Christianity and its break from Judaism.

Additional Text Resources

Maps:

The Kingdom of Israel (284)

Palestine at the time of Jesus (292)

The Jewish diaspora (296)

Paul's missionary journeys (302)

The spread of Christianity (312)

Document Extracts:

The Ten Commandments (287)

The Sermon on the Mount: The Beatitudes (298)

Charlemagne and Harun-al-Rashid (315)

Features:

Beliefs of Other Contemporary Peoples (289)

Spotlight:

Icons and Iconoclasm (310)

Chapter Eleven: Islam

Chapter Outline

A. Islam: Submission to Allah

    1. The *Quran* and the *hadith*

    2. The *hijra* and the *umma*

B. Perspectives on Islam: How do we know?

    1. The problem of sources

    2. Controversial issues: conversion, gender relations

C. The Prophet: his life and teaching

    1. Development of the Quran

    2. Muhammad: "Messenger of God"

    3. The Five Pillars of Islam

        a. monotheism

        b. prayer five times a day

        c. alms-giving

        d. fasting during Ramadan

        e. pilgrimage to Mecca

    4. *Jihad* and the *dar al-Islam*

    5. Women: debates over the effects of Islam

    6. Muhammad in war and peace

D. Succession struggles and the early caliphs

    1. Abu Bakr, the first caliph

    2. The first civil war and the Umayyad Dynasty

    3. The second civil war and divisions in Islam

        a. Shi'ites and Sunnis

        b. Twelver Shi'a and the "Hidden Imam"

    4. The heights and depths of the Umayyad Dynasty

    5. The third civil war and the Abbasid caliphate

E. The Abbasid Caliphate

    1. Stress in the caliphate

    2. Emergence of quasi-independent states

F. Islam Expands

    1. Ghaznavids, Ghuirids, and the Sultanate of Delhi

    2. Southeast Asia

    3. Almoravids and Almohads in Morocco and Spain

    4. Sub-Suharan Africa

5. Seljuk Turks and their sultunate

6. Mongols, Turks, and the destruction of the caliphate

G. Spiritual, Religious, and Cultural Flowering

1. Law: the *Ulama*

2. Sufis: mystics of Islam

3. Intellectual synthesis

4. The global transmission of technology

5. City design and architecture

H. Relations with Non-Muslims

1. Islam and the sword

2. The Crusades

3. Spain and the *Reconquista*

I. Conversion and Assimilation: How do we know?

Chapter Summary

This chapter forges an in-depth account of the Islamic faith from its inception in 570 C.E. when in fact, it dominated most of the Eastern Hemisphere.

Chapter Eleven begins by introducing the reader to the prophet **Muhammad**. As it is told, in 610 C.E., Muhammad heard the voice of the angel **Gabriel**. Over the next two decades, Gabriel proceeded to reveal **Allah's** messages to Muhammad. Recorded by a scribe, these messages were compiled into what is today known as the **Quran**– "...the absolute, uncorrupted word of God." According to Islam, in the chain of prophets, Muhammad is the "...last and final link."

Creator of the original Muslim community (**umma**), Muhammad established his authority in **Medina** and through an embittered dispute, succeeded in drawing the infamous city of **Mecca**, his hometown, under Isalmic rule. Despite unyielding Christian/Jewish factions, by the time of his death in 632 C.E., Muhammad was close to creating an Arabian-wide federation dedicated to the principles and political structure of Islam.

Following Muhammad's death, political leadership fell into the hands of what is known as the **caliph**, successor to the prophet and head of the Muslim community. Keeping a certain degree of "power in the family," the first four caliphs were all relatives of Muhammad himself.

The struggle for political, economic, tribal, and religious power initiated a series of civil wars at the dawn of the third caliph, **Caliph Uthman's** reign. As a consequence of such insurrections came the functional end of the caliphate, but not the spread of Islam. Regional rulers, finding themselves more independent, pursued politics of political and military expansion while proclaiming the religion and culture of Islam as their own. Muslim domination reached such areas as the **Indian sub-continent**, **Southeast Asia** (present day **Malaysia** and **Indonesia**), **Morocco**, much of **sub-Saharan Africa** and for a brief time, **Spain**.

Chapter Eleven goes on to discuss selected aspects of Islam, including law, culture, intellect, and the global transmission of technology.

In Islam, law supports the fundamental notion of **hisba**, "...to promote what is right and to prevent what is wrong." Encountering all aspects of life, legalities are of great importance to Muslim perpetuation. In the eighth and ninth centuries, the major systems of Islamic law were codified and such laws still endure today.

Islamic culture was distended through the conquest of new lands. For example, when the Muslims conquered **Iran** in the mid-seventh century, **Persian** became the second language of Islam.

Well noted in the history of Islam are a vast array of intellectual traditions, among which mathematics, astronomy, and medicine prevail. Islamic contributions in this arena include **algebra**, the concept "**zero**," herbal remedies, and a knowledge of pharmacology, just to name a few.

Concluding with a discussion of technology, architecture, and religious struggles, Chapter Eleven details the transmission of Chinese paper making throughout the Islamic domain, discusses the agricultural innovations that enriched Muslim society, describes the architecture of **mosques**, mausolea, and government buildings, and finally ends with an explanation of the **Crusades**.

Learning Objectives

After students have read and studied Chapter Eleven, they should be able to:

1. Describe the legal, political, and religious beginnings of Islam.
2. Locate on a map the areas into which Islam spread following the functional end of the caliphate.
3. Identify the Five Pillars of Islam.
4. Identify the legal, intellectual, and technological advances made by the Muslims in early Islamic history.
5. Identify the spiritual and cultural underpinnings of the Muslims in early Islamic history.
6. Identify the causes of civil strife amongst the Muslims in early Islamic history.
7. Describe early Islamic cities/architecture.
8. Discuss what role the Muslims played in the Crusades.
9. Describe the legal/social role(s) of Muslim women in the Islamic world.
10. Identify the figures: Muhammad, Gabriel, and Allah

Suggestions for Lecture Topics

1. Discuss the similarities and differences that exist between Sufi, Sunni, and Shi'ite Muslims. Describe the role each sect plays in the Islamic realm.
2. Present an in-depth look at the Five Pillars of Islam. Look at how each pillar affects the everyday practices of Muslims.
3. Discuss the role of the Muslim expansion/migration. Explain the mass introduction of Islam to various corners of the world.
4. Present an in-depth look at a woman's role in the Islamic faith. Examine both the positive and negative effects of Islam on her role in society.
5. Look at the face of Islam in today's day and age. What role do Muslims play in our world? Talk about anti-Muslim sentiment (i.e. terrorism, etc.).

Topics for Essays or Class Discussion

1. Discuss the rise and fall of the caliphate. What elements contributed to its emergence and subsequent decline?
2. Compare the emergence of the two subsequent monotheistic religions (Judaism and Christianity) with Islam. Do you see any parallels?
3. Look at Islam's contributions to the area of pharmacology. Cite specific innovations. How might the world be different without these?
4. Discuss Islam's contributions to the study of mathematics.

Vocabulary

Quran	monotheism
jihad	caliph
imam	dar al-Islam
mahdi	dhimmi
hajj	heliocentric
umma	hijra
Allah	Sufis
tariquat	hadith

Audio-Visual Resources

Islam: *Faith and Nations*: color.

This film discusses the fundamentals of the Islamic religion and the nations in which it is practiced.

Additional Text Resources

Maps:

The expansion of Islam (327)

The rise of the Delhi Sultanate (331)

Islam in south and southeast Asia (332)

Islam in Africa (333)

Byzantium and Islam (333)

The Mongol World (334)

The Empire of Timur (335)

Document Extracts:

Ibn Battuta's Observations on Gender Relations (347)

Features:

The Synthesis of Al-Ghazzali (339)

Mausolea in Islam (345)

Dhimmi Status (348)

Spotlight:

The Dome of the Rock (342)

Chapter Twelve: Establishing World Trade Routes

Chapter Outline

A. Trade and Traders: Goals and Functions

    1. World trade: <u>What difference does it make?</u>

        a. who benefited from world trade before 1500 C.E.?

        b. free market economies vs. "subsistence as a moral claim"

    2. Trade networks 1250 C.E. – 1500 C.E.

        a. scholars of trade networks: Janet Abu-Lughod and Eric Wolf

        b. the development of world trade networks before, at, and after 1500 C.E.

B. World Trade Patterns, 1100 C.E. – 1500 C.E. <u>What do we know?</u>

    1. The Americas

        a. Mesoamerica

        b. the Andes region

    2. Sub-Saharan Africa

        a. West African: the trading kingdoms

        b. East Africa and the Indian Ocean network

    3. Indian Ocean Trade

        a. ships of trade

        b. Jewish traders

        c. Muslim traders

    4. The military and trade empire of the Mongols

        a. Genghis Khan

             i. the extent of Mongol conquests

             ii. the Pax Mongolica

        b. World travelers: Marco Polo and Ibn Battuta

        c. bubonic plague and the trade routes

    5. China and South China Sea

        a. from Mongol to Ming: dynastic transition

        b. international trade and government intervention

             i. the voyages of Zheng He

             ii. the costs of limiting China's trade

    6. Medieval Europe and the Mediterranean, 700 C.E. – 1500 C.E.

        a. the early Middle Ages

             i. manorial economy

             ii. feudalism

    b. the High Middle Ages

      i. the rise of an urban middle class

      ii. the Church revises its economic policies

      iii. guilds and city-states confront rural aristocrats

      iv. economic and social conflict within the city

    c. the Renaissance

      i. Renaissance humanism

      ii. Florence

      iii. new technologies

    d. ironies of the 14th century: plague and war

  7. The Rise of the Ottomans in Eastern Europe

  8. Exploration and discovery

    a. Portugal: Prince Henry the Navigator

    b. Spain: the *Reconquista*

Chapter Summary

This chapter relates the establishment and the development of ancient trade routes as well as the patterns and philosophies of early economic systems. It incorporates different parts of the world (Americas, Africa, Asia, and Europe), as well as relevant timeframes and people.

The chapter begins by asking the question why people are interested in trading. It then progresses into the aspect of why people trade as a result of economic profit motive. This notion of early **capitalism** gave rise to the terms supply and demand, although the chapter does make certain that there was no evidence of a working supply and demand mechanism before the third century B.C.E. Interestingly, ancient traders in the Mediterranean were not out for individual economic profit, but rather for reasons of community self-efficiency.

Trade patterns in the early Americas consisted mainly of the **Incas** in the **Andes Mountains** whose peaks and valleys allowed for product differentiation in trading such items as **sweet potatoes, maize, squash, beans,** and **chili peppers.** Meanwhile, the **Aztecs** were in control of **central Mexico** and the **Yucatan peninsula** where a guild of traders called a **pochteca** carried on long distance trade, which grew steadily in the fifteenth century. The pochteca would lead a caravan hundreds of miles in order to trade, and were rewarded accordingly by the leaders of the Aztecs through means of higher social status.

In Sub-Saharan Africa, trade occurred and developed mainly by the introduction of the **camel** in the second to fifth century C.E. **Oases** provided the necessary watering points for **caravans,** and produced **dates** which became a major item of trade. African trade was dominated by three empires (**Ghana, Mali, Songhay**) who successfully merged and managed to keep major trade routes open without incident. Gold, slaves, and ivory moved north across the Sahara, while salt, dates, and horses moved south. East Africa traded mainly with **Arabia** and **India.** In return for spices, pottery and glass beads, East Africa traded ivory, skins, and slaves.

The chapter continues to explain the development of Indian Ocean trade, which involved greater Asia, including India, China, and Russia. Much of the Indian Ocean trade was established through the exploits of Jewish and Muslim traders. Information on Jewish traders resulted from the **Cairo Genizah** which is a repository of old papers documenting secular and sacred aspects of life, including trade. Muslims began trading due to the fact that Muhammed himself was a trader. Since Muslims are required to conduct a pilgrimage to Mecca, travel must occur, and therefore, trade began to flourish.

After **Marco Polo's** exploits in China with **Kublai Khan** from 1275 to 1295 C.E., the world continued on as usual until the outbreak of the **Bubonic Plague** in 1346 C.E., which resulted in the death of nearly one-third of the population of Europe. Trade declined, and not until the late middle ages when the manorial system rose to prominence, did trade begin to recover.

The chapter concludes during the **Renaissance** time period where the elite few began to dominate world trade, leading to many future conflicts.

Learning Objectives

After students have read and studied Chapter Twelve, they should be able to:

1. Describe a free market economy.
2. Define the relationship between supply and demand.
3. Locate the Andes Mountains on a map of South America.
4. Explain what a pochteca is.
5. Describe the role of Africa (sub-Saharan and East) in world trade.
6. Explain the relevance of Jewish Disporas.
7. Summarize why Muslims become traders.
8. Identify Marco Polo as a pioneer of trade in China.
9. Explain why the bubonic plague reduced world trade.
10. Describe the nature of the manorial system in Europe.
11. Identify the Renaissance as a cause for future wars.

Suggestions for Lecture Topics

1. In describing how trade occurred between ancient civilizations (e.g. Inca and Aztec) compare how tradable goods were transported, as compared to today's more advanced methods of trade.
2. Explain why trade was so important to ancient people and how that importance has carried over to us in the present day.
3. Discuss the role that Marco Polo played in world trade. Is he a great pioneer as is supported by legend, or is he more comparable to Christopher Columbus and the role he played with the native Americans?
4. Discuss the role that different religions had in establishing trade routes in certain parts of the world (i.e. Muslims and Indian Ocean trading).
5. Explain why cohesion, as in the case of African Empires like the Ghana, Mali, and Songhay, is important to the establishment and maintenance of trade routes.

Topics for Essays or Class Discussion

1. Compare the trade in the Americas (North and South) with that of Africa and Indian Ocean trade. What characteristics do they share? How are they different? Who controlled the trade?
2. How does the notion of capitalism and the law of supply and demand differ today than when trade was just beginning to prosper in the ancient world? How is it the same?
3. Methods of trade today differ greatly from those used in primitive times. Still, we see remnants from the ancient world still used today. Explain why some places in the world still use these ancient methods of trade as compared to today's more technologically superior methods.
4. Describe some of the problems that early traders encountered while trying to traverse foreign lands and how they eventually overcame these setbacks.

Vocabulary

free market economy	khan
supply	transhumance
demand	bubonic plague
networks	medieval
pochteca	manorial economy
sahel	guilds
savanna	Renaissance

Audio-Visual Resources

The Age of Exploration and Expansion: Centron Films. 17 minutes, color.

Additional Text Resources

Maps:

World trade routes (360)

Pre-Columbian America (362)

African kingdoms (364)

The Mongol successor states (370)

The routes of the Plague (372)

Medieval European trade (381)

Document Extracts:

Rights of the Poor: Subsistence as a Moral Claim (359)

The Fabulous Travels of Marco Polo (374)

"Capitulare de Villis"--Feudalism and the Rules of Manor Life (380)

The Origins of a Businessman: St. Godric of Finchale (383)

The Realpolitik of Niccolò Machiavelli (388)

Features:

St. Thomas Rationalizes the Practices of Business (384)

Spotlight:

The Ships of Trade (366)

Chapter Thirteen: The Unification of World Trade

Chapter Outline

A. Capitalism and the Expansion of Europe

    1. Capitalism: a definition

    2. European capitalism and the expansion of trade: <u>What difference does it make?</u>

B. Spain's Empire

    1. New World conquests

    2. Making the conquests pay

    3. Merchant profits

    4. Warfare and bankruptcy

C. Trade and Religion in Europe: the Protestant Reformation and the Catholic Counter-Reformation

    1. The Reformation

    2. The Counter-Reformation

    3. Religious beliefs and capitalist practice

    4. Protestant Challenges from the Dutch Republic and England

D. Portugal's Empire

    1. Sugar, slaves, and food

    2. The Indian Ocean: advancing Portugal's coastal explorations of Africa

    3. How significant were the Portuguese?

E. The Dutch Republic

F. France and England

    1. France: consolidating the nation

    2. Britain: establishing commerical supremacy

        a. British triumph in overseas trade: <u>What do we know</u> and <u>How do we know?</u>

        b. agriculture in economic growth

G. Capitalism

H. Diverse Cultures: Diverse Economic Systems

    1. Russia

    2. Ottomans and Mughals

    3. Ming and Qing Dynasties in China

    4. Tokugawa Japan

    5. Southeast Asia

Chapter Summary

This chapter explains the introduction of the concept of **capitalism** to the world, and its relationship to the European powers of Spain, Portugal, the Dutch Republic, France, and England, as well as the Asian powers of

Russia, the Ottoman Empire, the Mughal Dynasty, China, India, and Japan during the time period ranging from 1500 to 1776.

The chapter begins by giving a brief introduction to the concept of capitalism, then turns to European colonization and its role in the expansion of trade. Spain is the first power discussed, having become a world trade power through the wealth gained from its exploration of the New World. Spain reorganized the economies of the Americas through the **encomienda** system, **repartimiento** system, and the **mita** system–all three considered cruel to the citizens that lived under these systems. **Charles V** and his son, **Philip II,** were the two powerful Spanish kings of the sixteenth century. Charles V funded political programs in his European territories by using Spanish wealth (acquired mostly from the New World) which ultimately led to a revolt. Philip II maintained the policies of his father and, not surprisingly, had the same results.

The **Reformation** and its role in Eurpean trade is discussed with emphasis placed on **Martin Luther**, who claimed that the **Catholic curch** had too much power over individual conscience, **John Calvin**, who denied the authority of the Catholic Church, and **Henry VIII**, who wanted to head the **Church of England** himself and make divorce legal. The Catholic Church responded to this reformation with the **Council of Trent**. This **Counter-Reformation** was an attempt to re-establish the religious monopoly held by Catholicism. Despite this reaffirmation, **Protestantism**, now flourishing in individual nation-states that no longer wished to be associated with the vision of a world unified under the Catholic church, continued to set its own agenda by emphasizing individual achievement and grace. Nowhere was this emphasis more prominent than in **Max Weber's** *The Protestant Ethic and the Spirit of Capitalism*--which tied together the Protestant view of the individual with economic enterprise.

The chapter continues with an explanation of **Portugal's** empire and the **Dutch Republic**. Portugal utilized sugar, slaves, food, and the **Indian Ocean** to become a world trade power, while the Dutch developed the most efficient economic system in Europe.

The other two European Powers of the time were **France** and **England**, who were in constant competition with each other to establish themselves as the dominant trade power of the world. Each pursued a different strategy to achieve this goal, with France employing a land strategy and England employing a sea strategy. The two countries also chose different economic routes with the French embracing the concept of **mercantilism**, which fostered the economic welfare of one's own nation against all others, while England, through capitalism, was able to achieve a unified national market throughout its territories. The use of these strategies not only helped England prevail over France in their endeavor, but also subsequently led to the rise of capitalism in other European countries.

Diverse economic systems existed throughout the world, but **Russia** was at an extreme disadvantage because, for the most part, it was landlocked. Much of the more powerful nations' economies depended on a strong sea presence, and the only ports that Russia possessed were in the Arctic and, invariably, frozen for most of the year. The reign of **Peter the Great** helped to initiate economic growth in the country, despite its disadvantages. At the same time, the **Ottomans** and the **Mughals** became rising powers in the region of Asia who closely paralleled the rise and fall of Spain and Portugal. On the far reaches of Asia, **Japan** introduced a **shogunate**, or military, government.

The chapter concludes with a discussion of **Southeast Asia**. While the region was dominated by commerce, the merchants that benefited from this trade were, for the most part, foreigners. Native merchants rarely, if ever, participated in the trade industry. Subsequently, Southeast Asia became a victim of capitalism–while local rulers participated in it by entering into commerical agreements with foreign traders, the accumulated wealth rarely made its way back to the merchant communities, creating a serious imbalance of power and wealth.

Learning Objectives

After students have read and studied Chapter Thirteen, they should be able to:

1. Define capitalism, know its pros and cons, and its relationship to religious beliefs.
2. Compare and contrast the Spanish Empire to the Portuguese Empire, and explain the rise and fall of both.
3. Construct a time line of important events from 1500 – 1776 in relationship to world trade.
4. Explain the importance of the New World conquests.
5. Discuss the role of slavery in the world trade spectrum.
6. Explain the reformation and the views of Martin Luther, John Calvin, and King Henry VIII.
7. Describe the Counter-Reformation. Know the decisions made by the Council of Trent regarding Catholicism.
8. Locate on a map, territories controlled by the Spanish, Portuguese, English, French, and Dutch.

9. Explain the economic efficiency of the Dutch Republic.
10. Describe the state of France and England in the time period of 1500 – 1776. Compare the two countries and describe the conflicts the countries had with each other.
11. Explain the economic disadvantages faced by Russia. Know who and what was done to make up for these shortcomings.
12. Discuss the dominant trading powers in Asia.

Suggestions for Lecture Topics

1. Explain the meaning of capitalism and how it related to European expansion. Explain how this led to colonization.
2. Discuss the rise and fall of the Spanish Empire. Note Spain's role in exploring new land (i.e. Christopher Columbus). Also, note what kinds of products were valuable to Spain for trade. Discuss the role of the two powerful kings of the sixteenth century–Charles V and Philip II.
3. Explain the Reformation and the Counter-Reformation and their relationship to world trade. Discuss the views of Martin Luther, John Calvin, and King Henry VIII. Discuss the role of the Catholic church.
4. Discuss the Portuguese Empire. Note the importance of sugar, slaves, food, and the Indian Ocean. Refer back to the Spanish Empire and point out similarities and differences.
5. Explain the efficient economic system of the Dutch Republic. Note the actions taken by England and France to slow down the effectiveness of the Dutch economy.
6. Discuss the competition for world trade dominance between France and England. Discuss the two different strategies–France-by-land and England-by-sea–and why England won out. Discuss the histories of both France and England and how they relate to trade.
7. Discuss the differing economic systems of Asia--Russia, the Ottoman Empire, the Mughal Dynasty, China, and Japan. While discussing the Russian economic system, note the significance of Peter the Great.

Topics for Essays and Class Discussion

1. Compare and contrast the Spanish Empire to the Portuguese Empire and the role each played in the dominance of world trade. Explain the factors that led to each country becoming a world power.
2. What role did religion play in European trade? What effect did the Reformation and the Counter-Reformation have on Europe? What were the three major reforms in the Reformation and who was responsible for each reform?
3. What factors led to the rise of France and England as economic powers? Who ultimately became the dominant power?
4. Explain the concept of capitalism. What role did it have in the expansion of Europe? How did capitalism affect the trade industry?

Vocabulary

capitalism	development of underdevelopment
encomienda system	repartimiento system
mita system	haciendas
indulgences	mercantilism
Asiento	supply and demand
laissez-faire	monopolies
Shogun	Samurai
Chonin	

Audio-Visual Resources

Three Worlds Meet, Origins 1620; Bala Cynwyd, PA: Schlessinger Video Productions, 1996. 37 minutes, 22 seconds, color.

Explores human arrival in the New World, the Age of Exploration, and Spanish conquests.

Additional Text Resources

Maps:

World Exploration (398)

The Reformation in Europe (401)

The first European trading empires (406)

Indian Ocean trade in the seventeenth century (408)

British power in India to 1805 (415)

Document Extracts:

Don Quixote of La Mancha (404)

Features:

How Significant Were the Portuguese? A Historiographic Debate (407)

The Joint Stock Companies in Asia (410)

Agriculture in Economic Growth (416)

Spotlight:

The European "Other" in Art (412)

Chapter Fourteen: Demography and Migration

Chapter Outline

A. Demography: <u>What is it and what are its uses?</u>

B. Asian Migrations, 1250 – 1600

      1. The Ottoman Empire, 1300 – 1700

      2. India: the Mughal Empire, 1526 – 1750

      3. Akbar's reign: <u>How do we know?</u>

      4. Safavid Persia, 1500 – 1700

      5. China: the Ming and Manchu Dynasties, 1368 – 1750

C. Global Population Growth and Shift

D. Fernand Braudel and the *Annales* School of History

E. The Expansion of Europe, 1096 – 1750

      1. The "Columbian Exchange"

      2. The Antipodes: Australia and New Zealand, 1600 – 1900

      3. South Africa, 1652 – 1902

F. Slavery: Enforced Migration, 1500 – 1750

      1. How many slaves? <u>How do we know?</u>

      2. Reinterpreting the slave trade: <u>What is its significance?</u>

      3. The plantation system

G. Cities and Demographics

      1. Delhi/Shahjahanabad

      2. Isfahan

      3. Istanbul/Constantinople

      4. London

Chapter Summary

This chapter introduces the concept of **demography**, as well as discussing the **migration** of conquering groups in Asia, the Americas, Australia, and New Zealand. It also shows the effects of these conquests on the native populations of the lands conquered.

The chapter begins with a description of important demographers and how they examine populations in quantitative terms. They use components such as **age groups**, **gender**, **household size**, **life expectancy**, **birth rates**, **death rates**, and more. Demographers seek to understand and interpret patterns of change.

The chapter first focuses on the Asian migrations from 1250 to 1600. There are a number of dynasties existing at this time including the Ottoman Empire, founded by Turkish invaders, the Safavid, the Mughal, the Manchus of China, as well as the descendants of **Genghis Khan**, who began new dynasties in Central Asia.

The **Ottoman Empire** (1300 – 1700) grew from a small holding in northwest **Anatolia** to become a world power. The Ottomans confronted the **Habsburg Empire** in Central Europe. These two groups often clashed over territory and finally developed boundaries that still exist today. These battles exhausted the empire and ultimately halted its expansion. The empire eventually fell far behind Western Europe and Russian economically and militarily, effectively ending its reign as a world power.

The **Mughals**, a mixture of **Mongol** and **Turkish** peoples from Central Asia, began their conquest of **India** in 1526. The four generations of emperors dominated most of the subcontinent. They ruled from magnificent capitals in the north, and mobile tent cities in the south. The decline of this group came after their leader, **Auranzreb**, engaged them in extended military campaigns that exhausted resources.

The **Safavid** peoples (1500 – 1700) conquered and repopulated **Persia**. This group began to assimilate Persian customs, but found it difficult to unite the diverse peoples of **Iran**. By the end of the seventeenth century, the Safavid army was unraveling and Iran was in anarchy.

The chapter focuses next on **China**. In 1211, Genghis Khan conquered China, marking the beginning of the **Yuan Dynasty** (1271 – 1368) whose reign ended in disgrace when they were driven out by the **Ming**, who ultimately established their own long rule (1368 – 1644).

In the next section, the chapter analyzes population growth and shifts. The internal developments in Europe are then discussed to explain why power was in the process of shifting away from Asia. These factors include changes in the balance of trade, and increasing order in European armies. Demographers estimate that Europe's population more than tripled between the years 1000 and 1700, while, in the meantime, Asia's remained steady, Africa's declined (due to the removal of slaves by dominant trade powers), and America's declined due to the loss of the native population.

The chapter goes on to descripe European expansion, in which European rule would extend over three continents in addition to its own.

Australia and **New Zealand** were first explored by the Dutch in the 1600s. Not until 1768, with the voyages of **James Cook**, would the land be used by the British government as a location for its **penal colonies**. This coming of the European population destroyed the fragile ecology of **aboriginal** civilization with the introduction of disease.

Another area of the world that felt the effects of European conquest was **South Africa**. The British would eventually gain control of this area as a trade route, and would later take advantage of the native population by selling a great many as slaves all over the world. These groups, by way of forced migration, would populate areas everywhere as part of this profitable trade.

The chapter concludes with an examination of **rural** to **urban** movement. There is a comparison of the Asian and Eastern European capitals (with their decline in the seventeenth century because of political and economic factors), and London (which grew primarily because of economic factors).

All of the conquests and land discoveries decribed in this chapter illustrate the changes that occured in population and demographics during these times.

Learning Objectives

After students have read and studied Chapter Fourteen, they should be able to:

1. Describe the components demographers use to examine human populations.
2. Identify the causes for the decline of the Ottoman Empire.
3. Describe the reasons why Aurangzeb's rule of the Mughal Empire led to its downfall.
4. Explain why the Mughal emperor Akbar was a successful leader.
5. Describe how the Safavids assimilated into the Persian culture after the conquest of these peoples.
6. Identify the internal developments in Europe from 1500 to 1700 that contributed to the shift in the balance of power from Asia to Europe.
7. Explain the effects of European colonization of Australia and New Zealand.
8. Trace the evolution of the slave trade in Africa, starting with the colonization of South Africa.
9. Explain how the slave trade was beneficial for Africa.
10. Compare the Asian and East European capitals to London in terms of growth during the 17th century.

Suggestions for Lecture Topics

1. Define the concept of demography as well as introducing the students to some of the leading scholars in this field. Discuss how it is that demographers examine human populations. Be sure to emphasize that not all information is easy to find, and that demographers must sometimes rely on secondary sources, such as

travelers' estimates of population. Conclude this discussion with an emphasis on the importance of the demographer's statistics, which can often tell stories of fundamental structures and changes in human society.

2. Present the ascension of various empires in Asia from 1400 to 1750. These include the Ottoman Turks, the Safavid and Mughal Empires, the Manchus in China, and the descendants of Genghis Khan in Central Asia. Point out the manner in which all of these empires came to power, emphasizing the effects on the native populations. Discuss the common elements of all these empires. They were all very powerful at one point–conquering land near and far–and all declined from either military or economic exhaustion, as well as from rising ethnic conflicts. Use the specific stories of these empires to illustrate this relationship.

3. Point out Akbar's reign over India as part of the Mughal Empire in order to emphasize his accomplishments. As a Muslim ruler of a Hindu majority, he was faced with a potential conflict. Describe how he overcame this problem by encouraging syncretism and the mixing of groups. He established an administrative bureaucracy modeled on a military hierarchy that still exists today. Conclude this discussion with a description of how Akbar's administrative efforts helped demographers interpret the population later in history.

4. Discuss the internal developments in Europe that began the shift in the balance of power from Asia to Europe. Explain how sheer demographic force of numbers in European expansion in their worldwide colonization reflected and helped cause the shift in power groups. Asia's population remained steady while Europe's tripled in the years 1000 to 1700.

5. Trace the history of Australia and New Zealand's colonization. Describe the efforts this colonization had on the native peoples. Finally, show the similarities between this colonization and what occurred when the Americas were colonized.

6. Discuss the evolution of the African slave trade. Show the economic importance of this trade on the expansion of the sugar plantation system. Describe Curtin's demographic work with the actual number of slaves removed from South Africa, his thoughts on how the slaves were captured and by whom, and how slaves were obtained after the abolition of the slave trade. Finally, discuss the positive and negative effects that the forced migration had on the continent.

7. Detail the economic factors that allowed London to grow while Asian and Eastern European capitals such as Peking, Delhi, Ishfahan, and Istanbul all declined during the 17th century.

Topics for Essays or Class Discussion

1. What components do demographers use to examine human populations? What do demographers do when studying earlier periods which lack a systematic data collection method? How do they use these statistics to learn about the groups of people under investigation?

2. What were the common elements behind the ascension of the Ottoman Turks, Safavid and Mughal Empires, the Manchus in China, and the descendants of Genghis Khan in Central Asia? How did these conquests affect the native populations? Also, how were the conquerors affected by the natives? What were the common elements leading to the decline of these peoples? Describe how rulers, such as Akbar in India, were able to be successful. What implications does this have for us today, living in such a diverse world?

3. The colonization by Europe had widespread effects on the population in the Americas, Australia and New Zealand, and Africa. Describe the effects on the native populations as well as the global population. Describe the positive and negative effects on the African continent. Finally, as Europeans continued their colonization, their populations grew. What was happening to populations elsewhere and why?

4. Based on the information presented in the chapter, what kinds of conclusions can you draw about expansion in general? How are populations affected by this movement?

Vocabulary

Longue Duree	demography
Sufis	Janissaries
Rajas	syncretism
Colombian Exchange	Asientos
Maidan	Caravanserais

Audio-Visual Resources

Suleyman the Magnificent: **Metropolitan Museum of Art and the National Art Gallery of Art, Chicago, IL. 1987.**

A biographical film of Suleyman, Sultan of the Turks. Describes his life and contributions to the expansion of the Ottoman Empire.

Additional Text Resources

Maps:

Eurasian empires, 1300 – 1700 (433)

Ottoman and Mughal Empires, 1300 – 1700 (433)

British settlement in Australia, New Zealand, and South Africa (445)

The African slave trade (448)

Document Extracts:

Ibn Khaldun on Urban Life in the Fourteenth Century (455)

Features:

Fernand Braudel and the *Annales* School of History (440)

The Columbian Exchanges of Plants, Animals, and Disease (442)

Spotlight:

Slavery: The Plantation System (452)

Chapter Fifteen: Political Revolution in Europe and the Americas

Chapter Outline

A. Political Revolution: Introduction, Definition, and Common Characteristics

B. England's Glorious Revolution, 1688

    1. Philosophical rationales

    2. Hobbes and the "State of Nature"

    3. The Bill of Rights, 1689

    4. John Locke and the Enlightenment

    5. Government by property owners

C. The *Philosophes* and the Enlightenment in the 18th Century

    1. The *Philosophes* and their ideas

    2. Adam Smith and the "Invisible Hand"

    3. The Scientific Revolution

D. Revolution in North America

    1. Causes of the American Revolution

    2. The Constitution and the Bill of Rights, 1789 – 1791

    3. The first anti-imperial revolution

E. The French Revolution and Napoleon, 1789 – 1812

    1. Origins of the revolution

    2. Historiography of the French Revolution

    3. The revolt of the poor

    4. International war, the "Second Revolution," and the "Reign of Terror," 1791 – 1799

    5. Napoleon in power, 1799 – 1812

    6. The Napoleonic Wars and the spread of revolution, 1799 – 1812

F. Haiti: Slave Revolution and Response, 1791

    1. Toussaint L'Ouverture and the Haitian Revolt

    2. Abolition of slavery and the slave trade: historians debate the causes

G. The End of Colonialism in Latin America: Independence and Disillusionment, 1810 – 1830

    1. Revolts of the creole elites

    2. Mexico

    3. Brazil

    4. Paraguay: the new historiography

    5. After independence

    6. Religious and economic issues: neo-colonialism and economic dependence

Chapter Summary

This chapter discusses the political and social motivations that cause **revolutions** within societies. Dealing with unrest in Europe and the Americas, this chapter deals with the major themes and people that were responsible for revolution.

The chapter begins by describing what a revolution is and gives stipulations between different revolutions such as **political**, **social**, and **military**. These revolutions usually lead to violence because of the motivation by both the hegemony and the revolutionary elements within the society to maintain individual ways of life.

England's **Glorious Revolution** in 1688 created a standard for revolutions to come between future groups. **Thomas Hobbes** (1588 – 1679) challenged the necessity for the English monarchy. At the time of Hobbes' writing, England was in turmoil over the incorporation of the monotheistic state. These religious troubles, as well as economic problems, led to the removal and subsequent execution of **King Charles**. **Oliver Cromwell** seized power and ruled until 1658. However, he was unable to restore an effective government, and in 1660, the monarchy was restored.

England did not favor the Catholic church. Fearing the reinstitution of Catholicism, England confirmed **William** and **Mary** as the new leaders. Led by the rhetoric of **John Locke** (1632 – 1704), and the 1689 **Bill of Rights**, England was successfully able to limit the power of the monarchy. There could be no armies recruited, nor could any subject be arrested and detained, without legal process.

The **Enlightenment** period called for a greater interest in knowledge and less influence on faith. The men and women of this period were driven by the pursuit of knowledge, and an explanation of the workings of the universe.

The chapter continues with the revolution in **North America**. English settlers in North America assumed they shared the rights of all Englishmen. Continued repression by **King George** led the colonies to declare their independence in 1776. This revolution went further than the Glorious Revolution in that it eliminated the monarchy altogether. These colonies achieved all the rights they received in England, as well as freedom of religion, freedom of the press, as well as all the other stipulations under America's own **Bill of Rights**.

With the success of the **American Revolution**, France saw a chance to expand around the world. The power shifted in France to the urban merchants and the artisans of the guild class. This class wanted an end to the **feudal** period, and sought equal opportunity for all, thus starting the French Revolution in 1789. This **Third Estate** exhibited a great deal of power and forced **Louis XVI** from the throne, later beheading him. France then created a republic that stood strongly against counter-revolutionary actions. This period was known as the "**Reign of Terror**." **Napoleon Bonaparte** came into power and developed France into a huge military power in Europe. Napleon's ambition became his own downfall when his drive to conquer led to France's defeat by both England and Russia. So sound were his defeats, that he was exiled.

The quest for individual freedom in Europe led to revolutions all over the world. The people of **Haiti** (led by **Toussaint L'Ouverture**), opposed to French rule and the practice of slavery, revolted against their colonizers, expelling them from their country and declaring independence in 1804. This slave insurrection had far-reaching implications as slavery would be abolished in England, Cuba, Brazil and (after the Civil War) in the United States before the end of the century.

Latin America soon followed suit in this era of revolution. Between the period of 1810 to 1826, virtually all Latin American countries expelled their conquerors and became independent--a direct result of political insurrection in America, France, and Haiti.

Learning Objectives

After students have read and studied Chapter Fifteen, they should be able to:

1. Describe the reasons for the various revolutions from 1660 to 1789.
2. Discuss the effects that the Glorious Revolution had on the monarchy of England.
3. Explain how the American Bill of Rights differs from the English Bill of Rights.
4. Compare and contrast the social and economic theories presented by John Locke and Thomas Hobbes.
5. Explain the changes in belief systems created by the Enlightenment.
6. Explain the principles behind Manifest Destiny and how it was used by American settlers.
7. Describe how the American colonies' victory over the British led indirectly to the French Revolution.

8. Explain the Revolution of the Rights of Man and the Citizen, produced by the French National Assembly.
9. Explain why Napoleon's attempts to conquer England and Russia were unsuccessful.
10. Describe how Haiti was able to gain independence from France and the effects this had on the slave trade.

Suggestions for Lecture Topics

1. Why was feudalism replaced with the economic principles of capitalism, and what effects did this have on England and the United States? What are the major differences between the guild system and the free market system?
2. What side do you see yourself taking in the French Revolution? Would you have sided with Louis XVI or with the Third Estate? Why?
3. What were the major mistakes made by Napoleon in his attempts to conquer England and Russia? What could he have done differently? With the huge rise of nationalism, did Napoleon even stand a chance?
4. Why were the Bill of Rights so important in the creation of the American government and how do they compare and contrast to the type of government in England? Would the United States have continued to be a satellite of England without the Bill of Rights?
5. The revolution in Paraguay followed the steps of other successful revolutions. Why was this particular revolution unsuccessful? Were the outside forces too much for Paraguay to overcome? Why?

Topics for Essays or Class Discussion

1. Why was England's Glorious Revolution the starting point for future revolutions in Europe and North America?
2. This chapter discusses revolutions that were successful and some that weren't. Describe some factors that made some revolutions more successful than others. What outside forces affected these outcomes?
3. Why was the adoption of the Bill of Rights so important to the American colonies? What result did it have in distancing America from England? How does the Bill of Rights affect life in present day America?
4. Why was the elimination of the slave trade so important to the people of Haiti? Would Haiti have been able to gain independence without the elimination of the slave trade?

Vocabulary

Manifest Destiny	mestizo
Jacobins	Caudillismo
Divine Right	Enlightenment
philosophes	Concordat
econometrics	maroonage
Mazombos	

Audio-Visual Resources

The Revolutionary War: Discovery Channel, 1989. 300 minutes, color w/black and white sequences.

This film is a historical overview of the Revolutionary War. Presented are social, political, and economic factors that lead to the escalation of the war.

Additional Text Resources

Maps:

The growth of the United States (475)

The empire of Napoleon (484)

The revolution in Haiti (485)

Liberation movements in Latin America (488)

Document Extracts:

An Epic Verse of Latin America (491)

Features:

Scientific Revolutions (472)

The Historiography of the French Revolution (478)

An Early Critique of Economic Dependence (494)

Spotlight:

Francisco Goya: Revolutionary Reality and Rhetoric (492)

Chapter Sixteen: The Industrial Revolution

Chapter Outline

A. The Industrial Revolution: <u>What was it?</u>, <u>What was its significance?</u>

B. Britain, 1740 – 1860

    1. Revolution in textile manufacturing

    2. Capital goods: iron, steam engines, railways, and steamships

    3. Why did the Industrial Revolution begin in Britain? <u>How do we know?</u>

C. The Second Stage of Industrialization, 1860 – 1910

    1. New products and new nations

        a. steel and chemical industries

        b. electricity

    2. Factory production

    3. Warfare and industrialization

    4. Effects of the "Second Industrial Revolution" worldwide

D. Social Changes: the Conditions of the Working People

    1. <u>What do we know?</u> and <u>How do we know it?</u>

    2. Demographic causes and effects of the Industrial Revolution

    3. Winners and losers in the Industrial Revolution

        a. social and economic effects on the workers

        b. public health legislation

E. Public Reaction in Britain and Europe, 1800 – 1914

    1. Political responses in Britain

        a. the Reform Acts of 1832 and 1867

        b. Factory Acts and Chartism

        c. labor organization and Parliament

    2. Labor organization in Britain

    3. Labor organization outside Britain

        a. Karl Marx and theories of worker revolution

        b. Germany, 1870 – 1914

        c. the United States, 1870 – 1914

        d. France, 1870 – 1914

F. Competition among Industrial Powers: the Quest for Empire

    1. European pre-eminence and "social Darwinism"

    2. The Ottoman Empire: the "Sick Man of Europe," 1829 – 1876

    3. Southeast Asia and Indonesia, 1795 – 1880

    4. India, 1858 – 1914

5. China, 1800 – 1914

    a. the Opium Wars and the Taiping Rebellion, 1839 – 1864

    b. the Boxer Rebellion, 1898 – 1900

G. Africa, 1653 – 1912

    1. Egypt, 1798 – 1882

    2. Algeria, 1830 – 1871

    3. South Africa, 1652 – 1910

        a. Zulus, Boers, and British, 1816 – 1902

        b. Labor issues: coercion and unionization

    4. European explorers in central Africa

    5. The "scramble for Africa," 1884 – 1912

H. Motives for European Colonization: Differing Historical Interpretations

Chapter Summary

This chapter deals with the global consequences of **industrial expansion** and **imperialism** in the years between 1740 – 1914. The chapter begins by describing what exactly the industrial revolution was, and its significance, discussing not only the factories and workshops of production, but also the procurement of raw materials.

The years between 1740 and 1860 are usually considered the most crucial in the industrial revolution. It was during this time that **Britain**, which is generally considered to be the birthplace of the revolution, greatly expanded its **cotton textile industry**, its railway network–which ultimately became its principle method of transportation and communication–and its steam-powered fleet of ships, enabling it to project its productivity to the far corners of the globe.

A revolution in textile manufacturing enabled Britain to surpass **India** in the production of lightweight, durable cotton textiles. While Britain had traditionally manufactured woolen garments, **cotton** began to displace wool as the fabric of choice. The establishment of Britain as the dominant nation in the production of cotton textiles was a two step process. First, heavy tariffs and regulations were placed on Indian imports, while British inventors created new machinery that would make their cotton textiles superior to Indian textiles in both quantity and quality. The first such invention was the "**flying shuttle**," developed by **John Kay** in 1733, which enabled a single weaver to send a weaving shuttle back and forth across a loom without the need of a second operator. Another prominent invention, created by **James Hargreaves**, was the "**spinning jenny**," a device that could spin yarn mechanically. Eventually these, and other inventions enabled Britain to surpass India in productivity. By the turn of the century, British weavers using such devices as **Samuel Crompton's "mule**," or **Richard Arkwright's** steam-powered "**frame**," were able to produce in about 300 hours, the same amount of cotton yarn that it took Indian weavers 50,000 hours to produce (about 100 pounds). By 1820, cotton textiles made up almost half of Britain's exports.

Other industries also flourished in Britain during this time period. The **iron industry**, which had been established in the mid-1500s, was aided greatly by innovations in the mining of coal–used to heat iron ore–which provided it more abundantly and cheaply. **Henry Cort** devised a new process of stirring molten iron ore at high temperatures, which encouraged the use of larger ovens and integrated the process of melting, hammering, and rolling the iron into high quality bars. The increased productivity of the iron industry, along with the invention of the steam engine helped establish the birth of the railway industry. **George Stephenson** produced the first reliable locomotive, the **Rocket**, in 1829, which paved the way for the British railroad boom in the 1840s. Eventually, this boom crossed the Atlantic to the United States where it facilitated westward expansion.

The last half of the nineteenth century witnessed the outbreak of the "**second industrial revolution**," with principle advances coming in **steel**, **chemicals**, and **electricity**, and further development in shipping, banking, and insurance.

Despite all the increased productivity and profits for industries and those that owned and operated them, there was a downside. Many workers were displaced by machines, and those that remained, barely made enough to afford living conditions not suitable for animals. Friedrich Engels, in his account of living conditions titled *The Condition of the Working Class in England*, (1845), was horrified at the conditions and would later team up with **Karl Marx** in calling for a revolution of the workers. This call came in the form of the *Communist Manifesto*, a treatise which sanctioned the abolition of private property.

The last thirty years of the nineteenth century were marked by labor unrest in Germany, the United States, and France–tensions that made conditions favorable for Marx's "inevitable" proletarian revolution. While this would not occur until the early twentieth century in Russia, it was clear that workers all over the industrial world were ready for a change.

The latter part of the nineteenth century was also witness to unprecedented European **imperialism**, thanks in part to the industrial revolution which gave Western Europeans, especially the British, a sense of superiority over the colonized peoples. Russia had begun to spread across Siberia, while the United States had conquered much of the land to the Pacific. The European effort was concentrated in Asia, especially China and India. By 1880, with the use of **steamboats** and vaccines to combat malaria now in widespread use, colonization had penetrated much of Africa as the British, French, Belgians, Spanish and Portuguese each grabbed various pieces of the pie for themselves.

Learning Objectives

After students have read and studied Chapter Sixteen they should be able to:

1. Describe the industrial revolution and its significance.
2. Discuss why the industrial revolution began in Britain.
3. Describe working conditions in factories during the industrial revolution.
4. Explain political reaction to the industrial revolution in Britain and Europe.
5. Describe the competition among industrial powers.
6. Discuss the motives for European colonization.
7. Describe the evolution of textile manufacturing.
8. Locate Britain and other European nations on a map.
9. Describe the impact of capital goods such as iron, steam engines, railways, and steamships.
10. Discuss English Romantic poets and the conflicting image of early industrial life.

Suggestions for Lecture Topics

1. Point out what the industrial revolution was and why it began. Explain the reasons why it began in Britain.
2. Discuss textile factories and the inventions that helped change it. Describe the capital goods–iron, the steam engine, railways, and steamships–and their effect and influence on the world.
3. Describe the second stage of industrialization's new products and new nations including steel and chemical industries, electricity, and factory production.
4. Describe and discuss the social changes and the conditions of the working people. Include demographic shifts and changes, working conditions, and the laws that governed them.
5. Describe and explain political reaction in Britain and Europe at this time–the labor organizations that were formed, and the competition among the industrial powers, including rebellions that occurred.

Topics for Essays and Class Discussion

1. What are the characteristics of the industrial revolution? Why do you think it began in Britain and not in the United States? Do you think any type of revolution of this kind is in our future?
2. What inventions do you think were the most important in the revolution? Why?
3. If you were a leader during this time period, what changes and/or policies would you have called for?
4. Discuss what you think the world would be like today if it were not for the industrial revolution (Have fun and be creative).

Vocabulary

textile factory

spinning jenny

cotton gin

the "Rocket"

assembly line

water frame

power loom

charter

Romanticism

Maxim gun

Audio-Visual Resources

The Industrial Revolution: **Modern Talking Picture Services, 1986. 90 minutes, color with black and white scenes.**

Explains why the industrial revolution came to England first, and explains the major stages in the nation's economic metamorphosis. Describes the effects of the revolution on society, particularly the working class.

Additional Text Resources

Maps:

The industrial revolution (502)

European imperialism 1815 – 1870 (520)

The decline of the Qing dynasty (528)

European expansion in Africa (532)

Document Extracts:

Conflicting Images of Early Industrial Life: The English Romantic Poets (503)

Assertions of European Supremacy and Obligation (521)

"The Attack of the King Industry" (526)

Features:

Labor Organization and Parliament: Two Views of Their Relationship (515)

Spotlight:

Through the Camera's Lens (508)

Chapter Seventeen: Social Revolutions

Chapter Outline

A. Introduction: Political, Industrial, and Social Revolutions

B. New Patterns of Urban Life

    1. Government centralization, industrialization, and urbanization

    2. The conditions of urbanization: <u>How do we know?</u>

        a. Primary documents of the times

        b. Poets of the city: Baudelaire and Whitman

    3. "Urban Sprawl" – <u>How do we know?</u>

    4. The non-industrial, non-European city

C. Gender Relations: Their Significance in an Age of Revolution

    1. Gender and history

    2. The movement toward equality

        a. the French Revolution and women

            i. Condorcet: Olympe de Gouges

            ii. reaction in the *Code Napoleon*

        b. the nineteenth century

            i. Mary Wollstonecraft

            ii. the Seneca Falls Convention (1848)

            iii. John Stuart Mill (1869)

        c. the movement for women's suffrage

    3. Gender relationships and the Industrial Revolution

    4. Gender relationships and colonization

    5. Women's bodies and reform: India, China, Europe

D. Nationalism: <u>What do we know?</u>

    1. What is nationalism?

    2. French nationalism

    3. Nationalism in the United States

    4. Nationalism on the periphery of Western Europe: positive and negative faces of nationalism

    5. The rise of Zionism in Europe

    6. Italy and Germany

        a. Mazzini, Cavour, Garibaldi, and Italian unification (1831 – 1870)

        b. Bismarck, Prussia, and German unification (1848 – 1871)

    7. China and Chinese nationalism (1856 – 1911)

    8. Anti-colonial revolts (1857 – 1912)

E. Japan: From Isolation to Equality, 1867 – 1914

    1. The end of the Shogunate

    2. Policies of the Meiji government

    3. Restructuring government

    4. Restructuring the economy

    5. Urbanization

    6. Cultural and educational change

    7. Gender relations

    8. War, colonialism, and equality in the family of nations

        a. the Sino-Japanese War

        b. the Russo-Japanese War

Chapter Summary

This chapter discusses the alarming rate of growth of eighteenth-century cities. While most started with small scale **suburanization**, which was made possible by new railroad transportation systems and later, the automobile, this grew to large scale **urbanization** very quickly. Industrialization is seen as primarily responsible for urban growth in the nineteenth century–steam engines could be constructed anywhere, thus, the location of factories became more flexible than in any other time in history. As a result, more and more jobs became available to immigrants, farmers, artisans, and, perhaps most disconcerting of all, children.

In his book *The Growth of Cities in the Nineteenth Century*, published in 1899, **Adna Ferrin Weber** called attention to the gradual breakdown of barriers between city and country. He asserted the necessity of urban growth to absorb the surplus growth of rural population. Ultimately, Weber cited four specific reasons for the growth of cities. First, the general improvement in **public health regulation**, which contributed to improved longevity-- especially in densely crowded cities; second, the **agricultural revolution**, with the use of increasingly sophisticated machinery to replace dozens, even hundreds of workers, freed up a workforce, subsequently leading to a mass exodus to the cities; third, the **growth of government**, which became increasingly centralized in cities; and finally, **rising standards of living** and more opportunities in education, social interaction and amusement. Despite the increased benefits of urban living, it was not without its drawbacks. While the urban mortality rate had steadily declined, it remained substantially higher than the rural mortality rate. The expected length of life in England and Wales in the late nineteenth century was forty-seven years, this expectancy was significantly lower in the industrial city of Manchester where it was only twenty-nine.

Weber's work was pioneering in the fact that it spawned many critical studies on the phenomenon of urbanization. **Charles Booth** (1840 – 1916) conducted research in London between the years 1886 and 1903, visiting and interviewing thousands of working people, which culminated in the seventeen volume *Life and Labor of the People in London*. Ultimately, Booth's goals were more personal than Weber's. A relatively successful English businessman, he wanted to investigate the problem of the existence of poverty and squalor in the midst of wealth.

The multitude of empirical research invariably led to philosophical speculation. **Max Weber** (1864 – 1920) published a series of essays and books about the changes occuring in cities and their populations which eventually helped establish the field of sociology. More interested in its institutional structure rather than its economics, Weber posited that these cities were a new creation that, unlike their medieval predecessors, were less autonomous–embedded within a nation-state that controlled its life and politics.

Non-European cities in Africa and Asia, did not remotely resemble their European counterparts, even before the industrial revolution, because they functioned primarily as political, cultural, and religious capitals, not economic ones. The coming of the Industrial Revolution, with its increased emphasis on economics, and the coming into power of leaders of commerce only intensified this difference. The industry that did exist in this realm--in cities such as Bombay, Singapore, and Dakar--were usually in the hands of European colonialists. The benefits of these industries benefited only the wallets of the investors, their countries, and the small clusters of European residents that would live segregated from the native population.

Gender relations and their significance to revolutions of industry are stressed heavily in this chapter. The Enlightenment and political revolutions in France, England, and the United States, led to an increased emphasis on the individualism. The individual was to be judged not by heredity or group identity, but by his or her own merits. Apparently, women were not given such consideration–their worth was not determined by their merits or potential, but by their obedience to their husbands. In his *Commentaries on the Laws of England*, jurist **William Blackstone** expressed the principle that a married woman was to be represented by her husband in the matter of important personal and financial decisions. Napoleon reiterated this sentiment in his own 1804 Civil Code, which stressed a wife's obedience to her husband. Nevertheless, the French Revolution had given birth to the term feminism–a term coined by philosopher Charles Fourier (1772 – 1837).

Before the end of the century, two essays–**Marie Gouze's** *Declaration of the Rights of Woman and Citizen*, written in 1790 under the pen-name of Olympe de Gouges, and **Mary Wollstonecraft's** *A Vindication of the Rights of Woman*, written in 1792–had been published, expressing concern over the lack of women's rights and arguing for equal opportunities for all in education. Both essays, however, did little to change the status quo. Gouzes was seen as a subversive by the Jacobins, who condemned her to death for royalism and feminism and had her guillotined.

It wasn't until 1866, when English philosopher **John Stuart Mill** petitioned Parliament to grant women the right to vote, that women's issues were given serious political consideration. Even so, Prime Minister Gladstone rejected Mill's petition. Undaunted, Mill continued to argue for gender equality on moral grounds, particularly in his essay *The Subjugation of Women*, written in 1869, where he asserted that equality among adults was necessary for the maintenance of a healthy family life.

In semi-rural areas, the industrial revolution progressed somewhat differently than in urban areas. Unmarried women, often the daughters of farmers, made up a majority of the factory workforce. Pioneers such as **Francis Cabot Lowell** (1775 – 1817) went so far as to provide housing for the workers in his Waltham, Massachusetts cotton mills–a legacy that would continue after his death with the establishment of the town of **Lowell, Massachusetts**; named in his honor.

Economic depression, and the more prevalent use of newer heavier machinery took its toll on the female labor force. Many were displaced either by machines or by farmers or new immigrants. In these difficult times, the demands of the male work force took precedence over the female work force. While a factory owner could just as easily hire three female workers for the price of one male worker, industrialization helped to establish cultural standards in England and America of the male supporting the entire family, with any income a woman might bring home viewed as "**supplemental**." More and more women were brought back to the home–under the supervision of either husband or parents. Those women unfortunate enough to have been the primary income earners for their families would take domestic service positions, while others, in some cases, would earn a living as prostitutes.

Nationalism became a powerful force throughout the world during this time. National and ethnic identity became the primary force behind the changes that took place in the early nineteenth century. Following the leads of revolution in the Americas and France only fifty years earlier, Western Europe became the site of nationalism's new message. Revolts broke out in the Balkans in 1815, Greece won its independence in 1829, the Ottoman Empire all but dissolved with the establishment of the independent states of Moldavia, Wallachia, and Serbia, and the nations of Germany and Italy became unified. Ultimately, the dark side of nationalism reared its ugly head. Much of the nationalistic fervor manifested itself in the persecution of those different from the established ethnic or national identity. Anti-Semitism became rampant in Europe and as a result, **Zionism** was founded by Austrian journalist **Theodor Herzl** in 1897 in order to establish a safe homeland for Jews in the area of **Palestine**.

Asia did not remain static during this political and social upheaval. Beginning with the **Opium Wars**, continuing with the losses of **Korea** and **Taiwan** to the Japanese, as well as the **Boxer Rebellion**, China's national identity, currently under the control of the foreign **Manchu Dynasty**, and too often compromised by the European and Japanese powers controlling its port cities began to assert itself, culminating in the revolution of 1911.

Beginning in 1857, the years leading to the turn of the century were filled with anti-colonial revolt in both Asia and **Africa**. **India**, **Egypt**, **the Philippines**, the **Caucasus**, **Indonesia**, and southern Africa were all the scenes of native peoples seeking to throw off the yoke of their European colonizers.

The country that underwent perhaps the most radical change during this time is **Japan**, which, in the years 1867 to 1914, moved from isolation to full participation in the world of nation-states.

Learning Objectives

After students have read and studied Chapter Seventeen, they should be able to:

1. Describe how cities form and move from colonizing, to suburbanization, onto urbanization.
2. Explain the different characteristics and reasons behind the growth of world cities.
3. Discuss how cities in Europe differ from those in Asia or Africa with emphasis on industry.
4. Explain how the political and industrial revolutions that occurred between 1688 and 1914 were certainly "engendered" events.
5. Explain the process of "Women's Emancipation" throughout world history.
6. Describe how gender relationships affected the Industrial Revolution.
7. Summarize the importance of nationalism in the world during the time of the Industrial Revolution.
8. Describe how European nationalism differs from that of the United States.
9. Discuss Italy and Germany, emphasizing the similarities of the past and differences today.
10. Describe Japan, including its politics, reconstructing government, and past and present gender relations.

Suggestions for Lecture Topics

1. Explain the process of urbanization, putting emphasis on what urbanization is, and the different stages a country goes through to get to it. Discuss the different documents and individuals cited in the chapter as evidence to reinforce your explanation.
2. Discuss the emergence of the new discipline of sociology in world history and how it was used by Booth and others in the chapter. Then, describe how this discipline was used to study a city. Emphasize the importance of population growth.
3. Compare and contrast the two poems written about "The City" in the chapter. Discuss how the philosophy of a city can be very different coming from two individuals of different socio-economic status.
4. Explain gender relations and their significance in revolutions. Describe the historical movement toward equality. Explain how women played a major role in the establishment of industry. Apply their importance to colonization to the lecture as well.
5. Explain the term nationalism and describe the different types of nationalism across the globe. Discuss how nationalism is important in quenching a country's desire to expand industrially. Apply these to the nationalism fed to non-western countries such as China. Point out how it affected them.

Topics for Essays or Class Discussion

1. What specific characteristics do you see in a country that is beginning to develop industrially? Are there any characteristics? If so, explain them.
2. What is the difference between a commercial and a cosmopolitan city? What characteristics do each of these cities have?
3. How do you see gender relations being important in industrial revolution? Or is it important at all? If yes, give three reasons from the reading and support each one with your own observations.
4. What is nationalism and how does it apply to the spread of world industry? Give examples. Do you think nationalism is always a good thing?

Vocabulary

gendered	gender relations	Zionism
urbanization	feminist	plebiscite
metropolis	family wage	Eurocentricity
urban sprawl	domesticity	Samurai
poverty line	signares	Shogun
cosmopolitan	nabobs	Han
commercial	nationalism	Daimyo
public sphere	spiritual principle	Geisha
garden city	ideology	Sukiyaki

Audio-Visual Resources

Industrialization and Urbanization from 1870 - 1910: **1996. 35 minutes, color/black and white.**

Deals mostly with United States industrialization.

Additional Text Resources

Maps:

Town and environs of Singapore (545)

European empires in 1914 (556)

The unification of Italy and Germany (559)

The expansion and modernization of Japan (567)

Document Extracts:

Poets of the City: Baudelaire and Whitman (544)

"Declaration of Sentiments": Seneca Falls Convention, July 1848 (548)

Feminist Frustrations: Living in a "Doll's House" (549)

Features:

Fukuzawa Yukichi: Cultural Interpreter (565)

Spotlight:

Women's Bodies and Reform (552)

Chapter Eighteen: Technologies of Mass-Production and Destruction

Chapter Outline

A. Technological Systems

    1. Technology and technological systems: definitions

    2. Technological transformations in the twentieth century

        a. demographic shifts and population increase

        b. urbanization and migration

        c. domestic change

        d. energy

        e. warfare

B. World War

    1. World War I: 1914 – 1918

        a. origins of the war

        b. trench warfare on the "Western Front"

        c. the United States enters the war

        d. new weapons: machine guns, tanks, poison gas

    2. The Treaty of Versailles: 1919

        a. end of the Habsburg and Ottoman Empires

        b. Germany: war guilt and reparations

        c. the League of Nations

    3. Economic depression and the expansion of welfare between the wars

        a. causes of the depression

        b. economic and political effects in Britain, the United States, and Germany

    4. World War II: 1939 – 1945

        a. origins of the war

             i. Hitler and the Nazis in Germany

             ii. Mussolini and Italian Fascism

             iii. Japan and China

        b. the war in Europe and Asia

        c. technology in the war

             i. war production

             ii. the mobilization of women

        d. the horrors of war

             i. the Holocaust

             ii. the atomic bombs

C. The Leviathan State

    1. The military state

    2. The "military-industrial complex"

D. The Image of Humanity

    1. Gandhi on technology and "civilization"

    2. Picasso, Freud, and Yeats

    3. Elie Wiesel

E. International and National Institutional Planning: 1945 – 1990s

    1. The Cold War: 1945 – 1991

    2. The United Nations today

    3. Ecological issues

F. The Nation-State, International Organization, and the Individual

Chapter Summary

This chapter shows the development of **technology** throughout the twentieth century. The main questions it answers are, "What is a technological system?" and "Why is it more important?"

The chapter begins by describing the more meaningful contributions technology has made to life. Improvements in medicinal and biological health care have increased the quality of living throughout the world. Through the practices of health services and the development in **food productivity**, people around the world can receive treatment and food in more efficient ways. Philanthropic foundations and organizations helped to fund movements, such as the green revolution, to improve third world standard of living.

These changes have caused demographic shifts in **population**, such as lower **death rates**, higher **birth rates**, and **family planning** programs. Populations have also moved steadily into cities in poor countries and away from the cities in richer nations. Through multinational corporations, the **first world** countries are losing businesses to the cheaper labor in **third world** countries.

Huge developments in **transportation** and **communication** have been advanced by the influential power of the computer system. Computers control most systems in today's industry and the transportation and communication of people, goods, and services. The **World Wide Web** is making it probable that people will use their homes to "work, shop, bank, and communicate with friends and family."

Energy has become a highly valued commodity in today's society. Countries that have it benefit and those that do not, seek to get it. On top of the natural energy, **atomic energy** came into use in the twentieth century, sometimes to the detriment of society (**Chernobyl, Three Mile Island**).

The chapter then proceeds to describe the destructive aspects of technology that are demonstrated through warfare. The idea of MAD has plagued the twentieth century since the development of the **atomic bomb**. The twentieth century will be known as the century of war in the history of books because of the two world wars which were fought in the first fifty years.

Because of the economic competition, power struggles, and security aspects, the century opened with a world war. **Germany, Austria-Hungary**, and **Italy** were pitted against **France, Russia**, and **Britain**. This war saw the introduction of the **machine gun** and the **tank**. Also, trench warfare slaughtered hundreds of thousands of people. In addition, the Germans introduced **poison gas** and **submarine** warfare which quickly set the advantage in their favor. The U.S. became involved militarily in 1917, one year before the war ended. After the war, President **Woodrow Wilson's** speech included the famous statement, "to make the world safe for democracy." His urgings would end in another war. In the aftermath, reparations were demanded of the German state and much territory was taken. As a result, the U.S. became a creditor nation to Europe and to debts of Germany. In 1929, the U.S. **Stock Market** crashed, sending the world into a **Great Depression**. The end of this era saw **FDR** propose his **New Deal** bringing the U.S. out of the terrible state they were in.

These same reparations were a major reason that triggered World War II. When **Adolf Hitler** took control of Germany, he made moves to take back what he viewed as rightfully his. With the help of Italy and later Japan, the **Axis** powers went up against France, Britain, and Russia again. This war was worse than the first in terms of warfare. Though trench warfare was abandoned, tanks, subs, and aircraft were perfected. But, two horrors distinguished World War II from all others.

Warfare by the mass extermination of a group of people was introduced by Germany in their plan to obliterate the Jews. Six million Jews were killed by Nazi Germany in what has come to be known as the **Holocaust**. The other weapon of mass destruction was the atomic bomb. The ultimate form of destruction was dropped on **Hiroshima** and **Nagasaki**, Japan after the U.S. entered the war. Since then, debate has raged over whether they should have been implemented.

The next era saw the **Cold War** between the two remaining super powers, the USSR and U.S. Through movements to outdo one another, the USSR eventually crumbled and the Cold War ended in 1991.

The final section of the chapter discusses the attempts to build institutions to harness technology for humane uses. Many voices of reason and humanity have been heard in the twentieth century. **Mohandas Gandhi** advocated freedom for his country by non-violent means. New, abstract, native, and ethically inspired art forms showed the spirituality of cultures. Psychology and psychoanalysis came to the forefront by pioneers like Freud. First hand experience was shown through the works of **Elie Wiesel**, a Jewish survivor of the Holocaust.

Another attempt at rebuilding the world was by the development of the **United Nations** (UN). Originally designed to be a security council, the UN became directly involved in waging war and waging peace. The latter half of the twentieth century was spent on the latter. The UN was involved in organizing against global ecological destruction by targeting the depletion of the ozone layer, global warming, acid rain, etc.

The last attempt is the trend of developed and developing nations to form alliances, organizations, and coalitions to protect their economic, political, and military interests. Groups such as **OPEC**, the **EU**, and **OAS** are designed to protect the interests of the members. The future of the world is dependent on the success of the U.S., the European world powers, and the nations of China, Japan, and the Tigers of the Orient, to be discussed in the remaining chapters.

Learning Objectives

After students have read and studied Chapter Eighteen, they should be able to:

1. Define what a technological system is and why it is important.
2. List at least six different inventions or innovations that helped to improve life and health conditions around the world.
3. Explain the impact fossil fuel energy resources have had on twentieth century society.
4. Describe the impact technology has made on the practice of "waging war," (waging peace).
5. Explain the impact World War I and World War II had on America and Europe, especially Germany.
6. Describe the "image of humanity" discussed in the latter part of the chapter as the authors explain it as well as in your own words.
7. Summarize the purpose and function of the United Nations as it is today.
8. Explain the differences among international organizations of states and countries (e.g. EU, OPEC, NATO, OAS, OAU, etc.)

Suggestions for Lecture Topics

1. There have been many technological inventions that have impacted society. One of the most important has been the development of plastic. What impact has the development of plastics had on society? List some everyday things in which plastics are a vital asset. Describe some other items that have had a major impact on the twentieth century.
2. Do you think nuclear weapons were (are) a good idea? If you do, explain why there has been so much controversy surrounding their use. If you don't, describe some alternative means that would render their use unnecessary.
3. How have ecological issues changed the ways in which societies are run (governed)?
Or have they? Describe some different issues and what organizations are doing to help.

4. Now that the cold War has ended, do you see any need to continue funding the United Nations military? Explain your reasons.

Vocabulary

World Health Organization	Triple Entente	Archduke Ferdinand
DDT	Manhattan Project	Triple Alliance
Green Revolution	Treaty of Versailles	United Nations
counterurbanization	depression	Greenpeace
OPEC	New Deal	perestroika
MAD	Holocaust	glasnost

Audio-Visual Resources

The World in Conflict: 1929-1945. **Network Television Production, 1997. 26 minutes, color and b/w.**

The worldwide economic depression that followed in the wake of the stock market crash is most severe in the nations defeated during World War II. Inflation plagued the world, and Hitler rose to power with Nazis while Mussolini lead the Fascists. The communists added a third ideology for the future of the world.

The Modern World: 1945-1980. **Network Television Production, 1997. 26 minutes, color and b/w.**

The postwar reconstruction, called the Ax Americana, leads to the Cold War. China becomes a regional power and colonial wars erupted in Africa and Asia. The Space Program takes off and the human drive for exploration is reinforced.

The Modern World: 1945-1980. **Network Television Production, 1997. 26 minutes, color. and b/w.**

A straightforward account of the growth of militarism, the rise of colonial ambitions, and the diplomatic maneuvering that made global warfare all but inevitable.

Lest We Forget: A History of the Holocaust. **Logos Research Systems, 1996. CD ROM for Mac/Windows. Mac=11ci or better, 5MB free RAM; Windows=486 or better, 8MB RAM.**

Good overview of the Holocaust, its causes and effects. Each topic delves into more subtopics including the Weimar Republic, Nazi racism, and the Nuremberg trials.

Additional Text Resources

Maps:

World War I (584)

The new post-war nations (587)

World War II in Europe (590)

Document Extracts:

"How Should We Live?" (601)

Features:

Spotlight:

Chapter Nineteen: The Soviet Union and Japan 1914 – 1997

Chapter Outline

A. The Contrasting Experiences of Russia and Japan

B. Russia: 1914 – 1990s

    1. The build-up to revolution

    2. Lenin and the Russian Revolution

        a. the Revolution of 1905

        b. March and October revolutions, 1917

    3. State planning, 1920 – 1953

        a. Stalin's Five-Year Plans

        b. growth of Russian industry

    4. Women workers in the Soviet Union

    5. Exporting the revolution

    6. Russian state power and oppression

        a. Stalin's purges of the party leadership

        b. the "Gulag Archipelago"

    7. Khrushchev, Brezhnev, and Gorbachev

        a. de-Stalinization under Khrushchev

        b. Brezhnev and the arms race with the United States

        c. Gorbachev: *glasnost* and *perestroika*

        d. the collapse of the Soviet Union and the end of the Cold War

C. Japan: Fragile Superpower, 1914 – 1990s

    1. Before World War I

    2. Social consequences of wartime economic growth: the *zaibatsu*

    3. Militarism

    4. The run-up to the Pacific War, 1930 – 1937: Manchuria

    5. The Pacific War, 1937 – 1945

        a. the "Co-Prosperity Sphere"

        b. firebombing and defeat

    6. The Occupation, 1945 – 1952

    7. Continuities, 1952 – 1973: M.I.T.I.

    8. The "Oil Shocks" of 1973 and 1979

    9. International investment finance: 1989 – 1990s

    10. Social-economic-technological problems within Japan

        a. an aging society

        b. an overworked society

Chapter Summary

This chapter describes the history of **Russia** and **Japan** during the twentieth century, focusing on the technological path that each nation has taken and how these paths compare and have interacted. The first half of the chapter discusses Russia, and the second half discusses Japan.

The chapter begins by focusing on Russia's build-up to revolution, encompassing the years 1914 to 1917. Lagging behind other countries in terms of industrialization, **Nicholas II** made a concerted effort to help his country catch up. He helped increase industrial production, but while he effectively doubled the per capita level of industrialization, other countries like the United States had quadrupled theirs. What remained was sharp class divisions consisting of the wealthy elite and impoverished peasants. The climate was ripe for change.

The **Bolshevik Revolution**, under the leadership of **Lenin** was direct result of the economic hardships faced by the urban working and middle classes. Seeking to overthrow the **bourgeoisie** and other proponents of the status quo, Lenin and his followers successfully toppled the **Czar**, and emerged victorious from the civil war that followed.

Lenin's plans for the fledgling new government was massive industrial transformation. Unfortunately, he did not live to see his dream come to fruition, and leadership of the country was taken over by **Josef Stalin** (1879 – 1953). Stalin, like Lenin before him, sought massive industrial development. In 1928, he instituted a series of five-year plans, with the hopes that Russia would catch up to other industrialized nations. Ultimately, Stalin was successful, especially in light of the worldwide depression that was plaguing many other nations.

The industrial success led to a desire to spread this successful **communist** formula to other nations, especially those that still struggled to develop. This plan was in direct opposition to that of the United States leading to **Cold War** which lasted from the years following World War II, to the early 1990s.

The chapter next focuses on Japan. Tracing a technological and economic development from the beginning of the century to **World War I** under the **Meiji government**, a great deal of change takes place this time. Unprecedented economic growth resulted from Japan's ability to develop its industry as the rest of the industrial world was involved in World War I. This growth resulted in the establishment of wealthy cliques, or **zaibatsu**, that engaged in all forms of economic activity and, funded by self-sponsored banks, controlled much of Japan's economy. The influence they had on government policy helped to establish a shift to military industrialization, which resulted in less governmental control over the military.

In an almost neverending search for resources, and a buffer zone against Russia, the Japanese military, no longer taking orders from Tokyo, overran and took control of **Manchuria**, establishing the puppet state of **Manchukuo**, under the leadership of handpicked emperor **Pu Yi**. The Japanese civilian government could not reign in the increasingly brazen military, and soon fell.

A clash with Chinese troops near **Beijing** in 1937 marked the beginning of Japanese involvement in the Pacific theater of World War II. In September 1940, Japan allied itself with the **Axis Powers** of Germany and Italy, but instead of aiding Germany on the Russian front, Japan chose to remain neutral, favoring combined military action against East and Southeast Asia, and the Pacific, specifically, French Indochina. This Japanese strategy, known as the "Greater East Aisan Co-Prosperity Sphere" proved disastrous as United States troops, in a series of daring island-hopping campaigns, pushed back the Japanese army, culminating in the drop of the atomic bomb.

Japan's defeat in World War II was followed by a seven-year period of occupation, in which Japan reverted back to its emphasis on technological growth which remains to the present day, with specific case studies such as the oil shocks of 1973 and 1979–which display a weakness in the Japanese economy because of its reliance on foreign oil. The Japanese economic model, emulated by the "**Asian tigers**" Taiwan, Korea, Singapore, and Hong Kong, while wildly successful, is not without its weaknesses. Japan faces an overworked population, with many of its citizens working long hours and in constant fear of **karoshi** (death from overwork). Its population is also an aging one; the life expectancy in Japan is among the longest in the world, so it must come to terms with the reality that the workforce will shrink as the population continues to get older. In addition, while Japan and its adherents enjoyed unprecedented economic excess, their populations continued to live with limited freedom–a situation Japan has sought to rectify with the introduction of parliamentary elections after the occupation. The one obstacle that Japan continues to face is its relations with other peoples–the self-centered policies that enabled Japan to develop its own industry and economy will have to be opened up in order to function effectively in an increasingly global realm of business.

Learning Objectives

After students have read and studied Chapter Nineteen, they should be able to:

1. State the changes in the technological life of Russia and in Japan that occurred through the twentieth century.
2. Describe the government of Russia during the twentieth century.
3. Explain the role that the leaders of Russia had on their government and country during the twentieth century.
4. Discuss examples of the change in Russia's government and social attitudes toward their own history and changes.
5. Explain the path of technological changes that Russia took during the twentieth century.
6. List examples that display the philosophy of Japan on her path to technological development during the twentieth century.
7. List military events that occurred along Japan's timeline of the twentieth century.
8. Discuss the effects of the technological developments of Japan on her people.
9. Explain the path of technological changes that Japan took during the twentieth century.
10. Discuss why Russia, Japan, and other nations felt that a path toward technological growth was/is an important one.
11. Evaluate the strengths and weaknesses of the paths that both Russia and Japan have taken during the twentieth century.
12. Explain Russia and Japan's relationship through the twentieth century and specifically during the events of World War I, World War II, the Cold War, and the present day.

Suggestions for Lecture Topics

1. Discuss Marxism and how it is evident in the events of the twentieth century Russia.
2. Give background on the saying, "All roads lead to Rome" and discuss the significance of, "All roads lead to Moscow."
3. Discuss the Shinto religion and the significance on the emphasis of an emperor's divinity and "the leading role of Japan's samurai warrior elite" (p.630).
4. Explore the philosophies that guided the path of Japan's technological and industrial growth.

Topics for Essays or Class Discussion

1. Compare and contrast the history and technological developments of Russia and Japan during the twentieth century. Then conclude by evaluating which path was more successful.
2. What effect did Russia and Japan's government and culture have on the technological developments of each country?
3. Discussing World War I, World War II, and the Cold War, evaluate the validity of this statement: Okachi Masatoshi, as director of Japan's Institute for physical and chemical research in 1937, is quoted on page 630 as saying: "In the final analysis future wars will not be wars of military might versus military might. They will be wars involving the entire nation's scientific knowledge and industrial capacity," (Morris - Suzuki, p. 127).

Vocabulary

communism	Marxism	zemstvo
mirs	duma	Cheka
collectivized	kulaks	NATO

glasnost

satellite nations

Shinto

perestroika

kamban

keiretsu

CIS

zaibatsu

technopolises

Additional Text Resources

Maps:

East Asia since 1945 (609)

Post-war Europe (619)

The break-up of the Soviet Union (626)

World War II in the Pacific (632)

Document Extracts:

The Gulag Archipelago (622)

Features:

"The Return of History" (624)

Economics in the Comic Books (628)

Historical Revisionism in Japan (635)

Controlling Pollution (636)

Spotlight:

Soviet Socialist Realism (620)

Chapter Twenty: China and India

Chapter Outline

A. Introduction: "Nation-Worlds" Compared

B. China, 1911 – 1990s

    1. The 1911 Revolution: Sun Yat-sen

    2. Power struggles, 1925 – 1937: Chiang Kai-shek (Jiang Jieshi)

    3. Mao Zedong and the Rise of the Communist Party

        a. Mao and peasant revolution

        b. gender issues

        c. the Long March and the rise to power, 1937 – 1949

    4. Economic revolution, 1949 – 1966: the "Great Leap Foward"

    5. The "Great Proletarian Cultural Revolution"

    6. Economic recovery, 1970 – 1990s

        a. Deng Xiaoping and industrial growth

        b. the "Four Modernizations" (and #5 "democracy?")

    7. China and the world, 1950 – 1990s

C. India, 1914 – 1990s

    1. The Indian National Congress and the independence struggle, 1914 – 1947

    2. New political directions and reform: Mohandas Gandhi

        a. Gandhi's philosophy and tactics

        b. Opposition to Gandhi's views in India

    3. India's problems and Gandhi's programs

        a. Hindu-Muslim unity

        b. abolition of untouchability

        c. cultural policies: maintenance of Indian cultural traditions

        d. prohibition (of alcohol)

        e. technology and its dangers

    4. The debate over technology: Gandhi vs. Nehru

    5. Independence and after

        a. "balkanization" – Pakistan and Bangladesh: the Punjab

        b. socialism vs. capitalism

    6. Gender issues

    7. Economic, social, and technological change since independence: seven problems

    8. International relations since 1947

Chapter Summary

Chapter Twenty focuses on the development of **China** and **India**, "The Giant Agrarian Nation-Worlds," through the twentieth century. The author details their respective struggles for self-rule in the first half of the century, while continuing with the social, political, and economic changes in each country up to the present day. His research spans up to 1997, using it to report, compare and contrast both modern China and India.

This chapter starts by discussing the first half of the century in China. In 1911, Chinese civilians revolted against the **Q'ing dynasty**, who had officially lost the "**Mandate of Heaven**." In 1949 **Mao Zedong** and the Chinese **Communists** won the Civil War and created the **People's Republic of China**, the first centralized government in China in over thirty-eight years. In between these two momentous events, China fought with issues of class struggles, gender issues, nationalism vs. foreign interference, and agrarianism vs. modernization in an atmosphere of war and chaos.

From 1949 on, the author focuses on the People's Republic of China and its struggle between enacting Communist principles and providing for the needs of the Chinese people. Disasters in economic planning during "**The Great Leap Forward**" led to the chaos of "**The Cultural Revolution**." In 1966, Mao demanded that the citizens revolt against authority and incite revolutionary spirit. As a result, the Cultural Revolution destroyed much of what China needed to be successful. Namely, agricultural growth, industrial production, and intellectual development. When the Cultural Revolution ended, the government faced new challenges. To face these challenges, **Deng Xiaoping** arose as a new leader by pushing them into more of a free market economy. Today, China is a rapidly developing country that holds 1/5 of the world's population. As it faces the future, questions of political freedom, economic freedom, population control, gender issues, global competition, and human rights constantly check its emerging influence as a developing country.

The focus on the chapter then switches to India; a country that fought for independence against their British colonizers until 1947. The oppressive methods of British political and economic control in India during the 19th and 20th centuries were increasingly being protested by such leaders as **Jawaharal Nehru**, **Muhammed Ali Jinnah**, and **Mahatma Gandhi**. The chapter pays particularly close attention to Gandhi, his political reforms, and *satyagraha* which was his peaceful and non-violent drive for *swaraj* (self-rule). As independence came in 1947, the issue of Muslim-Hindu tensions also came to a head, resulting in the partition of **Pakistan** that same year.

In the last half-century, independent India has mainly advocated socialism. Originally implemented under Jawaharal Nehru's leadership, his children (who succeeded him in leadership) have fit this socialist ideal in with an open market for India. The role of women in Indian society has widened in these latter years, yet many customs are still dictated by religious belief. Even in more recent times, India still experiences religious tension as seen in the partition of **Bangladesh** in 1971.

In more recent decades, India, like China, has undergone a process of rising out of third-world status by opening up their economy to other countries and thus, other cultures. In so doing, they seem to be "moving decisively into active participation in the world economy."

Learning Objectives

After students have read and studied Chapter Twenty, they should be able to:

1. Discuss the meaning of the term "Third World" by showing how it has been applied to China and India.
2. List the causes leading to the 1911 revolution in China led by Sun Yat-sen.
3. Explain the meaning behind each of Sun Yat-sen's "Three Principles."
4. Describe Jiang Jeishi's efforts to unify China under the Goumingdang (GMD).
5. Trace the history of the formation of the Communist Party in China up to their victory in the civil war of 1945-49.
6. Describe the events leading up to and resulting from the Cultural Revolution of 1966-69. In so doing, focus on the "Hundred Flowers" movement and the economic situation created by the Cultural Revolution.
7. List several reforms implemented in China by Deng Xiaoping since 1978.
8. Describe the social and economic practices of Britain as they ruled over the colony of India during the first half of the twentieth century.
9. Explain satyagraha, paying particular attention to its roots in Mahatma Gandhi's experiences in South Africa and its influence on Gandhi's political reforms.
10. Discuss the need for appropriate-scale technologies in relation to India and China and their domestic growth.

11. Trace the issue of the Muslim-Hindu conflict throughout the twentieth century.

Suggestions for Lecture Topics

1. Discuss what is meant by the term "Third World." First, show it was originally used as a positive label for countries striving to revive from colonization. Then, show how the term gradually acquired a negative connotation. Finish the lecture by showing how China and India can be considered "Third World" countries, and focus on their rising status in the global economy.

2. Explain the preconditions for China's revolution against the Q'ing government. Begin the lecture with a brainstorming session on the meaning of this quote: "In the official's house, wine and meat are allowed to rot, but on the roads are the bones of those who starve to death." Describe the Q'ing dynasty and why they were losing control over China by the twentieth century. Also, include the theme of foreign intervention in China by powers like the British, French, and the Dutch. Events like the Opium Wars and the Boxer Rebellion will help explain China's disdain for foreign interference at this time.

3. Present Marxism in its literal form. Discuss its relation to capitalism and its appeal to people throughout history. Explain why Communism appealed to the Chinese in the 1920s. Then, show how, according to Marxism, conditions were not right in China to implement Marxist Socialism. Conclude the lecture by showing how Mao changed Marxist theory to personally fit the lifestyle of the majority of Chinese people, ultimately leading to the People's Republic of China established in 1949.

4. While directing the class, explore the issue of human and political rights in China. Here, images of the Cultural Revolution should be brought up (the picture on page 657 in the book may be used). Also, the "liberation" of Tibet in 1959 should be discussed; highlighting the views of such contemporary figures as the Fourteenth Dalai Lama. To present both sides of the issue, be sure to note the rising economic tide in China and how it has created an increase in living standards. Note their geographic and population restraints as the People's Republic of China tries to manage Mainland China. Finally, conclude the discussion by exploring the assertion that free-market systems tend to promote basic human rights. Here, Nike's presence in China can be used as an example.

5. Trace the evolution of resistance against the British by the Indians in the early twentieth century. Discuss Britain's economic and political practices in regards to its colonies and how it was forced to give Indian citizens an increasing amount of control in their affairs. Here, it would be good to read from literature like "White Man's Burden," by Rudyard Kipling to explore the perspective of the British. In turn, bodies like the INC (Indian National Congress) should be discussed while focusing on leading figures that emerged out of it. Leaders like Mohammed Ali Jinnah, Jawarharal Nehru, and Muhatma Gandhi should be discussed and their philosophies examined. Also, describe events like the Armritser Massacre (1919) and how they effected the Indian drive for independence.

6. Examine ideological developments in Western thought that caught on in the East, particularly China and India. To do this, focus on Sun Yat-sen's "Three Principles" and Gandhi's political reforms. Here, Sun backs the idea of democracy for China but does not want China to take the same path of modernization that Europe had taken. Gandhi, too, wished for a more egalitarian society, but was against the use of English as the basic language in education and regional literature. Discuss why both advocated some Western practices while at the same time discarding others. Conclude the lecture with a discussion of the legacy of Western ideals on Eastern cultures.

Topics for Essays or Class Discussion

1. In light of China's and India's struggle for self-rule in the first half of the twentieth century, discuss the validity of this quote from Mao Zedong: "Political power grows out of a barrel of a gun."

2. How did Mao Zedong alter pure Marxism so that it would apply to China?

3. Compare and contrast the views of Mao Zedong and Mahatma Gandhi on issues of gender equality.

4. What are the advantages/disadvantages of a colonial power introducing and enforcing their educational system and values on their subjects?

Vocabulary Terms

agrarian

Jawarharal Nehru

Sun Yat-sen

Armritser Massacre

Jiang Jeshi

Untouchables

The Long March (1934-35)

patrilocal

Mahatma Gandhi

1911 Revolution

Indian National Congress

Mao Zedong

swaraj

Soviet

patrilineal

Tibet

Third World

Mohammed Ali Jinnah

communism

satyagraha

May 4th Movement

Pakistan

guerrilla warfare

Bangladesh

Audio-Visual Resources

A Passage to India: 1984. 163 minutes, color.

E.M. Forster's intimate portrayal of the tensions between the British and the Indians in the British India before World War I.

Additional Text Resources

Maps:

World population distribution today (646)

The Communist revolution in China (652)

Political change in South Asia after 1947 (672)

Document Extracts:

Gandhi's First Experience with Racism in South Africa (663)

Features:

First World, Second World, Third World (645)

Spotlight:

Appropriate-scale Technologies? (664)

Chapter Twenty-One: The Arab World and Its Neighbors

Chapter Outline

A. The Middle East and North Africa: Outstanding Issues

B. Turkey

    1. The end of the Ottoman Empire: Mustafa Kemal

    2. The rise of secular nationalism in Turkey, 1923 – 1990s

        a. Ataturk and modernization

        b. government alteration between democracy and military dictatorship

        c. NATO membership and western alignment

C. Egypt

    1. British rule, 1882 – 1952

        a. the *Wafd* vs. the Muslim Brotherhood

        b. Nasser and non-alignment

    2. Technological innovation, 1956 – 1990s

        a. the High Aswan Dam project and the Suez Crisis, 1956

        b. Egypt and Israel

        c. problems and progress in Egypt today

D. The Persian Gulf: Oil, Religion, and Politics

E. Iraq, 1939 – 1990s

    1. the *Baath* Party and Arab Socialism

    2. Saddam Hussein

        a. the Iran-Iraq War, 1980-88

        b. invasion of Kuwait and the Gulf War, 1990-91

F. Iran, 1970 – 1990s

    1. Shah Reza Pahlavi and modernization

    2. the rise of Ayatollah Khomeni

        a. the Islamic Revolution, 1979

        b. Iran and the world, 1979 – 1997

        c. Islamic law and domestic policies

G. Saudi Arabia

    1. Ibn Saud

    2. OPEC and development

    3. moderation in foreign policy

H. North Africa: Algeria

    1. The movement toward independence

    2. The Algerian Revolution and after

I. Israel

    1. Israel and the Arab World: <u>How do we assess significance?</u>

    2. The creation of Israel, 1948

    3. The Arab-Israeli conflict

Chapter Summary

This chapter focuses on the nations of the **Middle East** and **North Africa** which constitute the **Arab** world. Although the history of this region has evolved from the struggles against **colonialism** and **neo-colonialism** to the struggle to maintain government stability in these nation-states, it is ultimately, the discovery of **oil** in the region, various religious and political disputes, the establishment of **Israel** in 1948, and the intervention of outside states in the region that have dominated the politics of the region.

The chapter begins with the introduction of **Turkey**, the last remnant of the **Ottoman Empire** after its defeat in World War I by the French and British. According to the **Treaty of Sèvres**, much of the empire's heartland was to be carved into several areas to be controlled by **France** and **Italy**. Furthermore, an independent **Armenian** state was to be established in eastern Turkey on the shores of the Black Sea. To add insult to injury, a portion of Turkey was to fall under the jurisdiction of **Greece**, the centuries old Christian enemy of the Muslim Turks. Turkish general **Mustafa Kemal** (who later changed his name to "**Atatürk**") refused to capitulate to this legislature and led a rebellion against the terms of the treaty. He subsequently drove foreign troops out, which led to complete chaos between Turks, Greeks, and Armenians. Thousands of Armenians were killed in skirmishes in eastern **Anatolia**, signalling the death knell for the proposed Armenian nation-state. This slaughter was the third in the span of 25 years–the first coming in 1894 at the hands of the Ottoman Empire, and the second (and most brutal) occurring in 1915, with hundreds of thousands (perhaps as high as 1.8 million) of ethnic Armenians being massacred as potential "enemy sympathizers." In 1922, Kemal forced the sultan of the Ottoman Empire to abdicate, making Turkey a constituional republic. The 1923 **Treaty of Lausanne** legislated full recognition of the Turkish republic.

Upon gaining power, Kemal, now Atatürk (meaning "Father of the Turks"), implemented a number of reforms which, for the most part, meant a conversion to "Westernism." He replaced the Islamic calendar with the Gregorian, converted to the Roman alphabet, abolished the caliph, changed the city names of **Constantinople** and **Ankara** to **Istanbul** and **Angora**, and demanded that each Turk adopt a western style surname instead of the traditional Arabic personal titles. Ataturk hoped that this westernization would help Turkey begin the process of modernization and industrialization–making it more independant and self-reliant.

Egypt, while generally considered to be culturally the most sophisticated of all the Arab nations, has yet to experience the same economic and industrial explosion that occurred in Turkey. Soon after freeing itself from the yoke of Ottoman rule through the efforts of military governor **Muhammad Ali** (1805 – 1848), Egypt found itself under the control of the British Empire. This subjugation would last about 75 years, from the late-nineteenth century until 1956. During this time, Britain managed to reap the benefits of Egyptian cotton imports, and, most importantly, the **Suez Canal**, built in 1869, which effectively shortened the trade route between Europe and Asia.

Attempts to rebel against British rule were hampered both by British military might, and the lack of a unified front, as indicated by the myriad of "nationalist parties," that hoped to gain control of Egypt's fate. Eventually, two such parties emerged to the forefront, the secular **Wafd**, and the theocratic **Muslim Brotherhood**. While the Wafd won limited independence in 1922, as well as British withdrawal from the Suez Canal in 1936, much of the **ulama**, or scholars that decide on religous matters, were disenchanted by the Wafd's policies of constitutional government, secularism, and elective democracy. In fact, many of these religious figures preferred the continued rule of the British, where they were granted religious protection, to rule by the Wafd, who could, realistically, force secularization upon them. The government was eventually put into the hands of the Wafd during World War II under the rule of Khedive (King) **Farouk**.

In 1952, Farouk was driven out of Egypt by a coup and was eventually replaced by **Gamal Abdel Nasser** (1918 – 1970). He began bold programs of anti-imperialism and Arab unity. This led him to nationalize the Suez Canal, which led to an attack by Israel, Britain, and France to reclaim it. This attack was ended when the United States forced the countries to withdraw. Nasser launched many plans to socialize, industrialize, and modernize Egypt including many desert reclamation projects, and the **High Aswan Dam** (funded by the Soviet Union). His reign, however, was marred by the humiliating defeat his forces suffered in the **Six Day War** at the hands of Israel. After ordering United Nations troops out of their positions in the Sinai, he proceeded to blockade Israeli shipping through the Gulf of Iran, which led to a pre-emptive strike by Israel, resulting in the destruction of the entire Egyptian airforce and the loss of the Sinai, including the Suez Canal.

His successor, **Anwar Sadat**, was able (with the help of United States President Jimmy Carter) to negotiate a peace treaty with Israeli leader **Menachem Begin** which led to the return of the Suez to Egypt in 1979. After his assassination in 1981, **Hosni Mubarak** maintained Sadat's policy of peace with Israel. His authority, however, has been constantly challenged by religious militants (most notably the Muslim Brotherhood) who seek to make Egypt a theocracy.

Government instability dominates the political history of **Iraq**. After coups in 1948, 1952, and 1958 a struggle for dominance began among the high ranking leaders of the **Baath Party**–an Arab Socialist Party. This continued until 1968 when **Ahmad Hasan al-Bakr** established his military government. He was subsequently succeeded by **Saddam Hussein** in 1979. Hussein established his nation as the dominant military power in the Arab world, with over one-third of its gross national product allocated to military expenditure. His desire to control more oil resources and his fear of a potential alliance between Iranian Shi'ites and those in southern Iraq let to an eight-year war with Iran. Despite being backed by many Arab nations, who supplied him with weapons and money, and secretly supported by the United States, who wanted any nation other than Iran to hold supremacy in the region, Iraq was unable to win a decisive victory. Although almost 1,000,000 Iranians died in the war, Iraq had not made any substantial territorial gains.

Hussein's continued desire for oil led to his invasion of Kuwait in 1990. Again, he failed to make substantial gains because of the defeat of his military at the hands of a coalition force led by the United States and supported by Arab nations such as Saudi Arabia and Syria.

Iran has gone through perhaps the most radical change of any country in the region in the past 25 years. Originally under the rule of **Shah Reza Khan**, his pro-British son **Muhammad Reza Pahlavi** took over as Shah in 1941 after Khan's abdication. Exploiting his countries vast oil resources, he brought unprecedented wealth to the nation. When his prime minister **Muhammad Mussadeq** tried to nationalize the Iranian oil industry, United States and British backed Iranian soldiers, under the orders of the Shah overthrew him. With the Shah now in complete control of the nation's future, he embarked on a "westernization" plan in hopes of modernizing his country. However, much of this westernization was limited to those foreigners brought in to run the new Iranian technological industries. Opposition to his policies was kept in check by **SAVAK**, the brutal Iranian secret police. Ultimately, resentment against the Shah and the western nations that collaborated to keep him in power grew and eventually exploded in a 1979 revolution that overthrew the Shah and saw him replaced with **Ayatollah Khomeini**, who had been in exile in France. Khomeini implented the **shari'a**, or Islamic law. Women were ordered to wear the **chador**, and any legal decisions were made in accordance with the **Qu'ran**.

Despite the many attempts by the Arab world to put an end to European colonialism in the region, it would continue to play a strong role in the collective future of all of its inhabitants, both Arab and non-Arab. In 1917 the British government issued the **Balfour Declaration** which called for the creation of the state of **Israel** within the borders of the nation of Palestine as a homeland to the existing Jewish population who faced rising **anti-Semitism** in Europe. This declaration caused serious problems for the Arab population in **Palestine**, which at the time, outnumbered the Jewish population 10 to 1. What the Arabs perceived as yet another act of Western political interference, the Jews perceived as the rightful restoration of the homeland of their ancestors.

The atrocities committed against the Jews in World War II added a sense of urgency to those in favor of establishment of the state. After the United Nations partition of Palestine in 1947, Israel officially became a nation in 1948. Soon after its inception, Israel was attacked by its Arab neighbors, who wanted to drive any element of Western colonialism out of their land. This attack failed, as did others in the coming years. By 1967, Israel had occupied the West Bank of the **Jordan River**, and the **Gaza strip**–land previously allocated to the Palestinians in accordance to the United Nations partition. The Arab-Israeli conflict is still a divisive issue and long-lasting peace has yet to be achieved.

Learning Objectives

After students have read and studied Chaper Twenty-One, they should be able to:

1. Name the countries that make up the Arab world.
2. Name the dominant religion in Turkey.
3. Define the meaning of Atatürk.
4. Explain the significance of the Treaty of Lausanne.
5. Explain the importance of the Aswan Dam.
6. Summarize the events leading to Nasser's rule.
7. Identify why Sadat was assassinated.
8. Explain the events leading up to the Iraqi invasion of Kuwait.
9. Name the religious leader who took control of Iran in 1979.
10. Identify the oil cartel that caused oil prices to rise sharply in the mid-1970s.
11. Identify the movement that called for Jews to establish a homeland in Palestine.

Suggestions for Lecture Topics

1. Discuss the development of the Israeli state and its position in the world today. Be sure to include an explanation of current events and how they relate to this topic.
2. Discuss the reforms of Atatürk. Explain to the students how the Turkish people were affected by his reforms, and the problems they encountered in changing their way of life.
3. Since this chapter centers around the Arab world, explore with the students, the Muslim religion. Give them a brief introduction to Islam, and explain to them some of the traditional Islamic laws and customs as they are practiced in the region. This will help to give students a better understanding of the Islamic world.
4. Describe the treatment of the Egyptians by the British and concentrate on how native Egyptians were exploited by the British colonists. Use this as an example to show how colonialism exploited native peoples.
5. Discuss how oil was found in the Middle East and how it has affected the politics of the region. Concentrate on organizations such as OPEC and events such as the Gulf War.

Topics for Essays or Class Discussion

1. Explain why it is stated that Turkey does not fit a simple political or cultural category.
2. What steps did Nasser take to modernize Egypt? What were the outcomes of these steps?
3. What are some of the differences between Israel and its neighbors and how are these differences being played out in today's world?
4. Discuss Algeria's transition from French colony to independent nation and the struggles the native Algerians have had to endure during this transition.

Vocabulary

Atatürk	theocratic	shari'a
Treaty of Lausanne	Gamel Abdel Nasser	chador
Khedive	infitah	Hajj
Wafd	Sykes-Picot Agreement	pogroms
ulama	intifadeh	Zionism
Balfour Declaration	effendi	fellahin

Audio-Visual Resources

Middle East Peace Agreement: **West Lafayette, IN: Purdue University Public Affairs Video Archives, 1994. 35 minutes, color.**
Surveys the background and effects of the peace accord.

Additional Text Resources

Maps:

The Middle East since 1945 (680)

The end of the Ottoman Empire (682)

Israel and its neighbors (705)

Document Extracts:

Social Realities of Colonialism: Two Views (700)

Spotlight:

Islamic Architecture for Contemporary Times (696)

Chapter Twenty-Two: Sub-Saharan Africa

Chapter Outline

A. Introduction: Important Questions

B. To World War I: Colonialism Established

    1. European encroachment and resistance

    2. Economic investment

    3. Colonial administration

C. Colonialism Challenged, 1914 – 1957

    1. The world wars and the weakening of European control

    2. Origins of the independence movements: political and educational

    3. Seeds of discontent: social, cultural, and religious

    4. Pan-Africanism, 1914 – 1945

D. Winning Independence, 1945 – 1975

    1. British colonies: Ghana, Nigeria, Kenya

    2. French colonies

    3. Belgian colonies: the Congo crisis

    4. Portuguese colonies

    5. Southern Rhodesia (Zimbabwe)

E. South Africa

    1. The Union of South Africa (1910)

    2. *Apartheid*

    3. Nelson Mandela and the African National Congress

    4. F.W. de Klerk and the transition to majority rule

F. Evaluating the Legacy of Colonialism

G. Independence and After

    1. Internal politics

    2. Altering borders

    3. Refugees and exiles

    4. Dictatorship and corruption

H. Economic Issues

    1. Socialism or capitalism? – searching for an African path to development

    2. Roots of the economic problems: an economic and historiographic debate

    3. Economic solutions

I. Cultural Life

    1. *Negritude*

    2. Music

    3. Cinema

    4. Literature

J. African History: <u>How do we know?</u>

Chapter Summary

This chapter focuses on the years of European colonialism in **sub-Saharan Africa**, African struggle with **colonization**, and the events since its independence. The chapter focus revolves around government and economics but does seek to develop an understanding of the struggle the African people faced as a culture as well as devoting a specific segment of the chapter on the South African **apartheid** system, which was overthrown in the 1990s.

The chapter begins by discussing **European** expeditions in pursuit of **commercial resources**, **tropical products**, **religious expansion**, and the prospect of claiming land for European control. Colonization took place soon after the **Berlin Conference** of 1884 – 85, which was held to negotiate claims to African land. Little concern for native inhabitants of the continent led to uprisings and opposition. These were quickly quelled by military forces sent in by the colonial rulers. Ultimately, the African continent would be divided among European nations and would be slowly influenced by **western technology**, **transportation** and **international trade**, thus setting the stage for a dominant **minority rule** over the native majority.

The profitability of the **colonial system** grew in spite of the native Africans. Exploitation of the land, soil erosion, inhumane treatment of the people including overwork and underpayment led to native rebellion and ultimately forced many people to return to their traditional subsistence farming techniques. Consequent colonial profitability was in jeopardy and tensions began to rise between colonial rulers and the native population. The text then suggests a change in world perception of Africa after **Mussolini's** invasion in 1935–effectively putting an end to continued colonization. Between 1914 and 1957, many countries were given the right to independence.

The chapter continues with the struggles of the native people's pursuit of independence, considering the lack of educated leaders and the diversity of the population. Newspapers and other technologies were soon implemented as means of promoting independence and served as propaganda for establishing political movements and parties. In addition, a discussion of the rise of African leaders against the colonial tyranny is marked by **Pan Africanism** and conferences, which would be held to call for an end to racism and inequality in Africa.

With the emergence of African leaders, independence soon followed for many countries beginning with the **Gold Coast**, which would be renamed **Ghana**. Unlike the **British**, who were willing to give up their colonies, **France** and **Belgium** were not so eager. Attempts at **assimilation** and even military control led to riots and chaos in the colonies. One by one, European rule left Africa and by the 1980s, **South Africa** remained the only white-ruled country south of the Sahara. Restrictive laws established apartheid, which would put limits on blacks in the country. Resentment would soon follow and **African National Congress** (ANC) leader **Nelson Mandela** would be imprisoned. Front-line nations would begin to shelter ANC leaders, while sanctions against South Africa by the United Nations would eventually lead to its independence in 1993. This marked the end to colonial sub-Saharan Africa but its dark legacy still lingers today.

Learning Objectives

After students have read and studied Chapter Twenty-Two, they should be able to:

1. Explain the economic, religious, and political reasons for European interest in sub-Saharan Africa.
2. Discuss the term monoculture and its implications on the environment and the people of sub-Saharan Africa.
3. Discuss the Nnamdi Azikiwe's influence on revolutionary journalism in Africa, and the effects of his work.
4. Describe the "great strikes" of West Africa including their reasons for doing so as well as the implications of the strikes.
5. Summarize the implications of the five pan-African meetings between World War I and World War II.

6. Discuss apartheid: what it was, the restrictions it made, and the political party that opposed it .
7. Evaluate the effects of colonialism on sub-Saharan Africa.
8. Explain the economic issues faced by many of the newly independent African countries.

Suggestions for Lecture Topics

1. In discussing the section on European interest in sub-Saharan Africa, explain why Europe was interested in the continent. Point out that they disregarded the population already inhabiting Africa and considered them savages. Along with capitalizing on the resources of the continent, Europeans wanted to "reform" the natives and teach the religious customs of the West.

2. Explain the horrid conditions Africans were forced to live in when working for the colonies. Give careful concern to the working conditions in the mines and the railroads, expressing the reasons for the people's uprising against the tyrannical colonial rulers. Consider the excerpt of Ousmane's novel, *God's Bits of Wood*, which can serve as a primary source of information in your discussion.

3. Discuss apartheid, and explain the effects it had on the everyday lives of the black workers in African cities. Continue the discussion by introducing Nelson Mandela as the leader of the African National Congress (ANC), and his role in ending apartheid. Be careful to discuss his prison term and the astonishment of the nation when after being released just two years prior, he becomes the president of South Africa. Finally, discuss his speech to the court at the Rivonia Trial, 1964 and his position as one of the oppressed.

4. Present the effects of colonialism on sub-Saharan Africa, explaining both the positive and negative effects it had on the continent. Pay careful consideration to the boundaries established by the colonial rule and the implications of those boundaries after independence.

5. Point out the difficulties sub-Saharan African countries had in searching for an appropriate form of government. Explain the problems many countries faced with dictatorships. Suggest the question of whether democracy as we know it in the United States would be effective in a country like Ghana.

Topics for Essays or Class Discussion

1. If one nation does not utilize its natural resources, do you think it is right for another nation to come in and capitalize on those resources? What if the world as a global society needs those resources to function?

2. Pretend you are a lawyer and you must defend the actions of the colonial rulers in sub-Saharan Africa. How would you plead your case?

3. Capitalism was a challenge in sub-Saharan Africa. What might a country do to make itself more capitalistic and understanding the culture and the environment, could the countries in sub-Saharan Africa effectively produce a capitalist economy? Support your answer.

4. Compare apartheid in South Africa with the treatment of African-Americans in the United States prior to the 1960s. How are they similar? Draw comparisons on the reactions of both groups of people toward their oppressors.

Vocabulary

monoculture	animist
hegemony	guerrilla-warfare
neo-colonial	refugees
apartheid	statism
front-line	Cadre

Audio-Visual Resources

South Africa: Forging a Democratic Union: 1994. 28 minutes, color.

The video addresses the apartheid legacy in South Africa and the United States' role in helping the African Nationals make the transition toward democracy.

Additional Text Resources

Maps:

Africa in 1914 (711)

The decolonization of Africa (719)

Ethnic groups in Africa (726)

Document Extracts:

Nelson Mandela's Speech to the Court at the Rivonia Trial, 1964 (723)

"Prayer to Masks" (736)

Features:

Traditional Institutions and National Governments (727)

Spotlight:

Refugees and Exiles (732)

Chapter Twenty-Three: Latin America

Chapter Outline

A. Latin American Diversity Today

B. Technology, Industrialization, and Latin American Elites, 1870 – 1916

    1. Foreign investments and primary production

    2. Immigration and social change

C. The Mexican Revolution, 1910 – 1920

    1. The dictatorship of Porfirio Diaz

    2. *Mestizo* revolutionaries: "Pancho" Villa and Emiliano Zapata

    3. Obregon and the revolutionary program

    4. Lazaro Cardenas: the revolution institutionalized

    5. Culture as a tool of revolution: Diego Rivera

D. Revolutionary Politics in the 1920s and 1930s: Peru and APRA

E. The Market Crash and Import Substitution, 1929 – 1960

    1. Import substitution (ISI)

    2. Militarism and democracy in Brazil, 1930 – 1990s

        a. Getulio Vargas and the "New State"

        b. Military dictatorship: "Order and Progress"

        c. Return to democracy

    3. Populism and nationalism in Argentina, 1920 – 1980

        a. Juan Peron and the *decamisados*

        b. Opinions from and about "Evita"

F. The United States and Latin America

    1. "Dollar Diplomacy" military interventions, 1898 – 1934

    2. Guatemala, 1951 – 1990s

    3. Chile, 1970 – 1990

    4. Cuba, 1950 – 1990s

        a. Fidel Castro and the Cuban Revolution

        b. Che Guevara and guerrilla warfare

        c. Cuba, the United States, and the Soviet Union, 1961 – 1991

G. Current Issues and Trends

    1. The military in power, 1960 – 1990

2. Economics and technology

    a. "development" vs. "growth"

    b. the crisis of the 1980s

    c. NAFTA

    d. environmental issues

3. Amerindians: oppression and response

4. Religion and hope for the poor

    a. "Liberation Theology"

    b. the growth of evangelical Protestantism

5. The "Unorganized Sector"

Chapter Summary

This chapter relates the search for international policy on economics and technology in Latin America, also comparing and contrasting the different countries–geographically located in **Central** and **South America**–from 1870 to the 1990s.

Beginning with Latin America's current diverse populations, the chapter discusses the ethnic origin of many of the half-billion people that make up this twenty-seven-country region. Approximately one-third of Latin Americans are **Brazilian** (about 165 million people), while one-fifth are **Mexican** (about 100 million). While about 300 million of its inhabitants speak **Spanish**, there are substantial portions that speak **Portuguese** (in **Brazil**) and indigenous Indian languages. Religiously, the region is overwhelmingly **Catholic** (about 90 percent), although many Protestant evangelical efforts are slowly affecting that percentage.

The population, for the most part, has flocked to large cities like **Mexico City** and **São Paulo**, while the rural population has remained steady at 100 million through the second half of the twentieth century. Cities now hold up to 75 percent of the region's population--up from 20 percent at the turn of the century. Contributing to this mass exodus has been the lack of work in the agricultural industry, where more and more jobs are becoming mechanized.

The industrialization of Latin American began, with Great Britain's financial assistance in the late-nineteenth century, and continued, under the watchful eye of the United States through the end of World War I. By 1919, **Argentina** alone had received, in a span of about fifty years, almost $10 billion in foreign aid and investments–half of which came from Great Britain. This was a catalyst for its **beef industry**, which, with the help of such innovations as ocean shipping with refrigerated compartments, and new railway lines, enabled Argentina to profitably export its wares to Europe. A by-product of this beef boom was the fencing off of the great plains, or **pampas**, into ranches–thus relegating the once free-roaming **gauchos** to ranch hands.

As industrialization began to take shape in Latin America, Mexico was in a state of chaos. The **Mexican Revolution** had begun in 1910 and would last until 1920. Urban and rural leaders rose up against dictator **Porfiro Díaz** and his policies which greatly aided the middle and upper classes, but decimated the lower classes of rural peasants and urban workers. Two hundred Mexican families owned about 25 percent of the nation's land, while foreign investors owned another 20-25 percent, leaving very little for the rest of Mexico's citizens. Some properties spanned over 13 million acres, with much of the land going unused, while peasants went hungry. Upon Díaz's abdication and subsequent exile to **Paris**, a powerplay arose for his vacant seat. Many of the candidates were **mestizos**–people of mixed race and culture calling for reform from the legacy of rule by the **creole elite**. Power constantly shifted hands through coup and assassination until the drafting of the **Mexican Constitution** of 1917. The leader at the time, **Venustiano Carranza**, was forced by the opponents he narrowly defeated to implement radical changes–geared toward the rights of Mexican workers–from the status quo.

While the revolution was occurring in Mexico, many of the problems that helped ignite it remained firmly entrenched in the rest of Latin America. The country of **Peru** was still plagued with discrimination against Indians, the poor, and a denial of this discrimination by its hegemony. In forming the **American Popular Revolutionary Alliance** (APRA) in 1924, **Víctor Raúl Haya de la Torre** hoped to put an end to these inequities, but following the Peruvian election of 1931, which the APRA seemed to be on the verge of winning, government forces imprisoned de la Torre and killed many of his followers.

The worldwide stock market crash of 1929 caused a decline in demand for many of the products which served as the only exports–coffee from **Colombia**, bananas from **Ecuador**, and tin from **Bolivia**. This resulted in a call for a new economic and technological policy called **import substituting industrialization** (ISI), which was called attention to the need of Latin American countries to diversify their productivity in order to ultimately decrease their dependence on the demand of foreign markets. Further industrialization took place during World War II, but did not lead to self-sufficency, as the leaders had hoped, for it required the import of new machines and technology-- not possible during the war years.

The chapter continues with a discussion of the complex relationship between the United States and Latin America. Although there had been much American investment in these countries–40 percent of all American foreign investment went to Latin America–there was a span of about 35 years when the United States would constantly send troops into these areas, most often to collect debt. These countries, with their reliance on a single tropical fruit as the basis of their economies, and their subservience to United States policies, were often referred to as **banana republics**. The relations were further muddled by the United States' support of the brutal Nicaraguan dictator **Anastosio Somoza** (1896 – 1956). Anti-government sentiment in Nicaragua had reached a point in 1979, where his dynasty was overthrown by freedom fighters known as **Sandinistas**.

Perhaps the fiercest conflict between a Latin American country and the United States took place in **Cuba**. Cuba had been under the rule of American supported dictator **Fulgencio Batista** (1901 – 1973) until 1959 when **Fidel Castro** and his anti-government forces, succeeded in capturing the capital and declaring a new government for Cuba. By forging close ties to Soviet bloc nations, Castro was implying his allegiance to **communism**, although this wasn't officially announced until December 1961. Those who had fled Castro's revolution hoped to return and restore the former government. With help from the United States, a number of these exiles embarked on an invasion of the **Bay of Pigs**–a military blunder that would almost ruin the presidency of John F. Kennedy. This action confirmed the position of the United States toward the new government of Cuba. In response, Cuba allowed the Soviet Union to position nuclear missiles on its soil, but quickly had them removed when President Kennedy threatened an invasion.

As Latin American countries adjust their economic policies, their standard of living is beginning to increase. While Latin America suffered from debt for most of the 1970s and 1980s, the North American Free Trade Agreement (NAFTA) along with the establishemnt of the free-trade zone Mercosor allowed the development of urban production centers at the countries' borders–although an increase in illegal narcotics distribution was also a by-product of this development.

Learning Objectives

After students have read and studied Chapter Twenty-Three, they should be able to:

1. Explain why some Latin American governments have offered new land to settlers.
2. Describe what happened in the Mexican Revolution from 1910 – 1920.
3. Summarize the stock market crash and how it affected Latin American economies.
4. Explain the "Good Neighbor Policy."
5. Discuss the "Dollar Diplomacy" and what it had to do with President William Howard Taft.
6. Describe JFK's "Alliance for Progress" program.
7. Explain the purpose for building the Trans-Amazon highway.
8. Discuss how social and economic changes of the twentieth century have transformed religious beliefs and practices.

Suggestions for Lecture Topics

1. Explain the conditions necessary for the development of technology and industries for the economy.
2. Point out the effect the stock market crash had on Latin America and the precautions taken to help these countries rebuild their economies in exporting and importing goods.
3. Discuss the Mexican Revolution and how it affected the people and leadership of other countries in Latin America. Why was there so much difficulty in meeting the needs of the people?

Topics for Essays or Class Discussion

1. Do you think history can be better portrayed through art rather than literature?
2. The PRI envisioned a one-party state in which a single party would include all the major interest groups and the contest for political power. Do you think this vision of the PRI can become a reality?
3. Who is Getulio Vargas and what did he accomplish while in Brazil?
4. What is the Monroe Doctrine of 1823, and what did it do for Latin America?

Vocabulary

pampas	Ordem e Progresso	haciendado
gauchos	estancias	Mercosur
Caudillo	Maquiladores	mestizos
fincas	Esatdo Novo	Ladinos
Descamisados	Liberation Theology	

Audio-Visual Resources

***Latin American Debt: Living on Borrowed Time?*: produced by Jim Wesley, directed by Joseph Camp, 1989. 29 minutes, color.**

This fim deals with the international relations of the United States and Latin America.

Additional Text Resources

Maps:

The economic development of Latin America (743)

Latin American politics in the twentieth century (754)

Features:

Opinions from and about "Evita" (758)

Che Guevara and Guerrilla Warfare (764)

The Political Economy of Latin American Development (767)

Rigoberta Menchu and Indian Political Organization (770)

Spotlight:

Diego Rivera: Muralist Painter of Mexico's History (750)